THE WORLD ALMANAC 2,501 INCREDIBLE FACTS FOR KIDS ON WORLD CUP SOCCER

EMILY J. DOLBEAR

WORLD ALMANAC BOOKS

Copyright © 2025 by Skyhorse Publishing, Inc.

All rights reserved. No part of this book may be reproduced in any manner without the express written consent of the publisher, except in the case of brief excerpts in critical reviews or articles. All inquiries should be addressed to World Almanac, 307 West 36th Street, 11th Floor, New York, NY 10018.

World Almanac books may be purchased in bulk at special discounts for sales promotion, corporate gifts, fundraising, or educational purposes. Special editions can also be created to specifications. For details, contact the Special Sales Department, 307 West 36th Street, 11th Floor, New York, NY 10018 or info@skyhorsepublishing.com.

Published by World Almanac Books, an imprint of Skyhorse Publishing, Inc.®, 307 West 36th Street, 11th Floor, New York, NY 10018. The World Almanac® is a registered trademark of Skyhorse Publishing, Inc. All rights reserved.

www.skyhorsepublishing.com

Please follow our publisher Tony Lyons on Instagram @tonylyonsisuncertain.

10 9 8 7 6 5 4 3 2 1

Interior design by Chris Schultz
Cover design by Kai Texel
Images by Getty Images, Shutterstock, and Adobe Stock unless noted.

Library of Congress Cataloging-in-Publication Data is available on file.

Print ISBN: 978-1-5107-8223-5
Ebook ISBN: 978-1-5107-8224-2

Printed in China

CONTENTS

Game On!	2
Who Rules the Pitch?	26
What Are the Rules Anyway?	44
Leaving It All on the Field	64
How to Be a World Cup Fanatic	82
The Road to the World Cup	100
Men's World Cup Stars	128
Women's World Cup Stars	144
Show Me the Money	162
Beyond the Cup	182
Index	200
About the Author	214

GAME ON!

30 TRUE THINGS ABOUT MEN'S AND WOMEN'S WORLD CUPS

1. World Cup soccer tournaments are held every four years.

2. A tournament every four years mirrors the Olympics, which inspired the first World Cup, held in 1930.

3. Host nations need time to prepare for millions of visitors. The qualifying tournaments and playoffs also take time.

4. The FIFA rules of the game are the same at men's and women's World Cup tournaments.

5. The women's World Cup tournament takes place the year after the men's. Or the men's World Cup tournament takes place the year before the women's, depending on how you look at it.

10

6. A trick to help you keep track: Women's World Cups are never held in even years. Men's World Cups are never held in odd years.

7. Soccer fans around the world get a two-year break from World Cup fever. Two years on, two years off.

8. All World Cup games have two 45-minute halves. That we know.

9. Referees almost always add minutes to the game clock. That we also know.

10. But since 2022, teams seem to be playing longer World Cup matches. The referee added a total record-breaking 24 minutes to the Iran-England group stage game due to goalkeeper injury. The first half had 14 added minutes.

11. Men's and women's World Cups have the same number of players per team and substitutions per game. One exception: In 2022, FIFA increased team size from 23 to 26 players and substitutions from three to five per game, due in part to Qatar's brutal heat.

12. All World Cups have mascots. What's not to love about a talking orange?

13. Footballers prefer a grass pitch over an artificial, or turf, field. The beautiful game is more beautiful on natural grass.

14. All women's and men's World Cup matches are now held on grass.

15. Brazil is the only nation that has competed in every single men's and women's World Cup tournament.

16. There is only one man or woman who has participated in more World Cups than anyone else: Formiga of Brazil. She played in her seventh and final World Cup in 2019 when she was 41.

17. The men's and women's World Cup champions are awarded different trophies.

18. The World Cup kicked off in 1930, with only 13 nations competing in Montevideo, Uruguay.

19. There was no World Cup in 1942 or 1946 because of World War II. Only 13 nations played in 1950, mostly for political or financial reasons.

20. The men's tournament expanded to 16 nations in 1954. It's been expanding ever since.

21. Here's a rundown of the number of nations that competed in all the men's World Cups since then: 16 (1954–1978), 24 (1982–1994), 32 (1998–2022), and 48 (2026).

22. Twelve nations competed in the first two Women's World Cups. That was in 1991 and 1995.

23. Here's a rundown of the number of nations that competed in all the Women's World Cups since then: 16 (1999–2011), 24 (2015–2023), and 32 (2027).

24. Every World Cup tournament has a host nation. Or sometimes two. Or even three.

25. The United States has been selected to host five times—the men's World Cup in 1994 and 2026 and the women's World Cup in 1999, 2003, and 2031.

26. The U.S. men's team has never won the World Cup.

27. The U.S. women's team has won the World Cup four times. They wear four stars on their jerseys.

28. Many retired World Cup players become sports analysts. Americans DaMarcus Beasley, Shannon Boxx, Clint Dempsey, Landon Donovan, Julie Foudy, Tim Howard, Alexi Lalas, and Carli Lloyd have shared personal stories and soccer insights on TV.

29. Americans love watching football (the other kind of football too).

30. More than 25 million Americans have tuned in to watch the World Cup finals for men and for women.

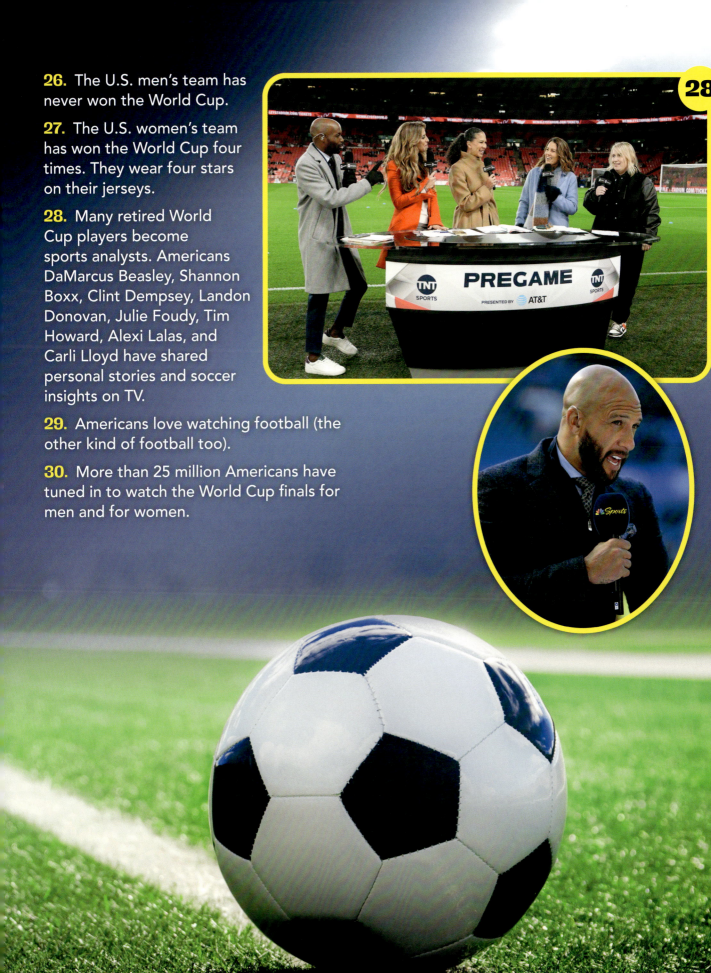

50 FACTS ABOUT THE ORIGINS OF FOOTBALL

1. Earth's most popular sport is football. The soccer kind, that is.

2. Over 250 million humans play soccer.

3. The sport has more than 3.5 billion fans.

4. People have kicked balls for centuries.

5. There were variations of the game in ancient Greece, Rome, and China.

6. They also played kickball games in Mexico and Japan.

7. More than 1,000 years ago, Japanese players kicked a deerskin ball between them. The purpose in *kemari* was not scoring but keeping the ball in the air.

8. The earliest footballs were hogs' heads. Try juggling that.

9. That's pretty gross for a game people call "beautiful."

10. The Chinese played kickball with a feather-stuffed ball.

11. In 16th-century England, football was a rough game played between villages. For a time, it was even banned.

12. William Shakespeare referred to the sport in 1594. In his play *The Comedy of Errors*, one character says, "That like a football you do spurn me thus?"

13. English settlers in Massachusetts wrote about an American Indian game played on the beach. It was called *pasuckquakkohowog*, or "they play with the foot," though ball handling might have been allowed.

14. Some men and women play professional beach soccer today.

15. Almost 400 years ago, a group of women in Scotland held an informal game of football on the village green after attending church.

16. According to a historic church document, the minister denounced the players. No football on a Sunday.

17. The minister didn't approve of their dancing either.

18. Modern football gained popularity in England. It was played in communities and at universities. But different rules often led to bedlam.

19. In 1863, the Football Association was founded in London, England, to address the problem of conflicting rules.

20. Local football club captains gathered in a tavern to draft official game rules.

21. It took six meetings and 44 days to complete the football rules.

22. The four British football associations later established the International Football Association Board (IFAB). Today, the IFAB sets and updates the Laws of the Game.

23. It was the Football Association who first officially called the game *association football*.

24. Association football was soon shortened to "assoc" or "soc" or "football."

25. In places where there's already football, like the United States and Canada, the sport is known as soccer. But you knew that.

26. In the 1880s, students at Cambridge University in England competed on organized teams with coaches.

27. A *New York Times* article from 1905 used the term "socker" in a headline. By 1910, the newspaper was regularly referring to "soccer fans."

28. The sport of football arrived in South America by way of sea travelers.

29. Sailors from Europe brought the game to Buenos Aires, Argentina.

30. British workers there founded the Buenos Aires Football Club in 1867.

31. The Buenos Aires Football Club was South America's first. Said a club founder: "I consider [soccer] the best, easiest, and cheapest pastime for the youth." Do you agree?

32. Members of the British military played soccer while stationed in Cape Town and Port Elizabeth in South Africa.

33. In 1896, a young Indian lawyer working in South Africa helped start a football association there. His name was Mahatma Gandhi.

34. Gandhi fought racism in South Africa.

35. Gandhi also led a peaceful revolution against British rule in India.

36. The name of Gandhi's football team? The Passive Resisters.

37. The first documented international soccer match took place in 1872 in Glasgow, Scotland.

37

38. England was set to play Scotland.
39. The match took place on a rainy Saturday in November.
40. Tickets to the match cost one shilling.
41. Kickoff was at 2 P.M.
42. Spectators numbered 2,500. Or 4,000, depending on who you ask.
43. Rules were vague, with no fouls, penalties, or cards.
44. Both teams packed their lineups with forwards. There were no subs.
45. Scotland wore dark blue, England white. Shirts were unnumbered.
46. Scotland apparently played a passing game while England preferred to dribble.
47. The first documented international soccer match ended in a draw, without a single goal. It happens.
48. The event was considered a huge success.
49. England and Scotland celebrated the event's 150th anniversary with a rematch.
50. England won the game, with goals from Harry Kane, Jude Bellingham, and Phil Foden.

50

SOME SOCCER JARGON:
30 FACTS ABOUT WORDS YOU THOUGHT YOU KNEW ALREADY

1. **Pitch** is the British word for a sports field.

2. A **kit** is a player's team uniform.

3. A kit includes shorts, cleats, shin pads, and socks.

4. And the **jersey**. That's the loose-fitting team shirt with the player's name on the back.

5. Your cleats are your **boots**.

6. A **cap** is each game you play for your country. And, yes, players receive a real cap for their first match.

7. The **box** is directly in front of the goal. It's also called the penalty area. This is where players are most likely to score.

8. A **screamer** is a powerful goal shot from a distance.

9. A **chip** is a short, high kick of the ball that goes over a defender's head.

10. A **sitter** is an easy scoring chance, usually in the box.

11. Missing a sitter is embarrassing.

12. Spice traders used to trick people by replacing valuable nutmeg seeds with bits of wood. Today, **nutmegging** means kicking a soccer ball through an opponent's legs.

13. Getting nutmegged is embarrassing.

14. When a player scores two goals in one game, it's called a **brace**.

15. English hunters still call a pair of birds or rabbits a brace.

16. If a player scores three goals in the same game, it's a **hat trick**.

17. A hat trick comes from another British game with 11 players—cricket. Cricket clubs used to award a new hat to bowlers who took three wickets from three deliveries in a row. (Bowlers? Wickets? Back to soccer, please.)

18. When a goalkeeper saves every shot on their goal, it's called a **clean sheet**.

19. Sports reporters used to record the score on white sheets of paper. The sheet was clean if no goals were scored by the final whistle.

20. Parking the bus means playing very defensively. Most of the team stays behind the ball on their half of the pitch.

21. It was Portuguese coach José Mourinho who first said of the other team: "They brought the bus and they left the bus in front of the goal."

22. Of course, teams that park the bus are much less likely to score—or get scored on.

23. Coaches use the "park the bus" strategy to defend a lead or secure a draw.

24. Flopping is taking a big fall or faking pain to draw a foul.

25. Diving is another word for flopping.

26. But you can also **dive** for the ball. If you're a goalkeeper. Ow!

27. Marking is closely defending a player.

28. A **knock** is a small injury you get during practice or a game.

29. Some people complain that a penalty or a yellow card is **soft**.

30. Soft means the call was too tough. Or just plain wrong.

27 FIFA FACTS AND A FEW FIGURES

1. FIFA (that's FEE-fah) governs international football, calling the shots for the game worldwide.

2. This global body promotes the sport and manages the world rankings of teams.

3. Oh, and FIFA also organizes the most prestigious international football tournament for men and women—the World Cup.

4. Some figures: the 2022 men's World Cup earned a record-breaking $7.5 billion, up *$1 billion* dollars from the 2018 tournament.

5. That whopping sum comes from broadcasting deals, sponsorships, and ticket sales.

6. Let's just say FIFA is one of the world's biggest sports organizations.

7. When it comes to global reach, soccer surpasses American football, basketball, or baseball.

8. FIFA headquarters are in Zurich, Switzerland, but there are offices around the world.

9. Next to FIFA headquarters is a full-size international football pitch.

10. In 1904, a French group founded FIFA in Paris.

11. F-I-F-A is short for *Le Fédération Internationale de Football Association*.

12. *Football association* is French for "association football," which we now also know as soccer.

13. It's not a fact but: Ever wonder what we'd call FIFA if the founders had spoken English instead of French? Maybe the *International Federation for Association Football*—IFAF. Or ISF, for the *International Soccer Federation*.

14. FIFA started with seven European countries. They were Belgium, Denmark, France, the Netherlands, Spain, Sweden, and Switzerland.

15. The eighth FIFA member, Germany, joined by telegram the same day as the other countries, but it's not considered a founding member.

16. England entered the federation in 1906.

17. The first FIFA member nation outside of Europe was South Africa.

18. Argentina and Chile signed up for FIFA in 1912.

19. The United States and Canada joined in 1913.

20. Today, FIFA has 211 member associations.

21. The United Nations started in 1945 with 51 countries to promote global peace and security after World War II. Now it has 193 member states.

22. How does FIFA have more members than the United Nations? FIFA admits nations that are not fully independent, such as Bermuda (a British territory).

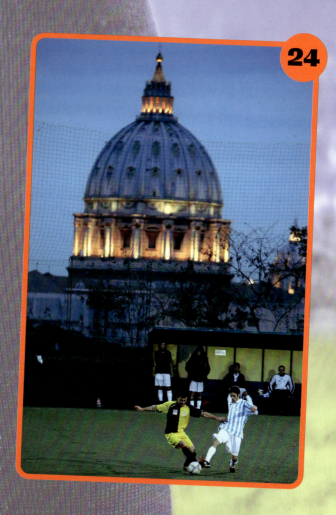

23. One spot in the world is not an official member of the United Nations or of FIFA: Vatican City, the city-state in the middle of Rome, Italy.

24. Home to only about 1,000 people, including the pope, Vatican City fields its own women's and men's teams. They play near St. Peter's Basilica.

25. The 211 FIFA-recognized national (men's and women's) soccer teams are working every day to reach the next World Cups.

26. One more fact about FIFA you should know: The organization also governs futsal and beach soccer.

27. Futsal is a fast-paced indoor version of soccer, with teams of five and a smaller ball.

62 MOSTLY ESSENTIAL FACTS ABOUT THE 1930 WORLD CUP

1. FIFA leaders voted to organize a World Cup just two years before the opening whistle. The goal? An international championship open to all member nations.

2. World Cup football would thrill spectators, surpassing even the Olympics.

3. In 1929, FIFA selected the host of its World Cup tournament: Uruguay.

4. The Uruguay team had impressed FIFA—and the world—by winning Olympic gold in 1924 and 1928.

5. Uruguay offered to pay for all the teams to come. The South American nation must have felt generous the year before its 100th independence anniversary.

6. Builders began construction on a brand-new stadium in the capital city of Montevideo. They had just eight months.

7. A Montevideo artist created a sleek, modern poster to promote the event. It showed a goalkeeper making a flying save.

8. All FIFA member nations were invited to the tournament. (This World Cup was the only one for which teams did not have to qualify.)

9. England was opposed to the World Cup from the get-go. They were no-shows.

10. Italy, the Netherlands, Spain, and Sweden weren't interested in participating after not being selected to host.

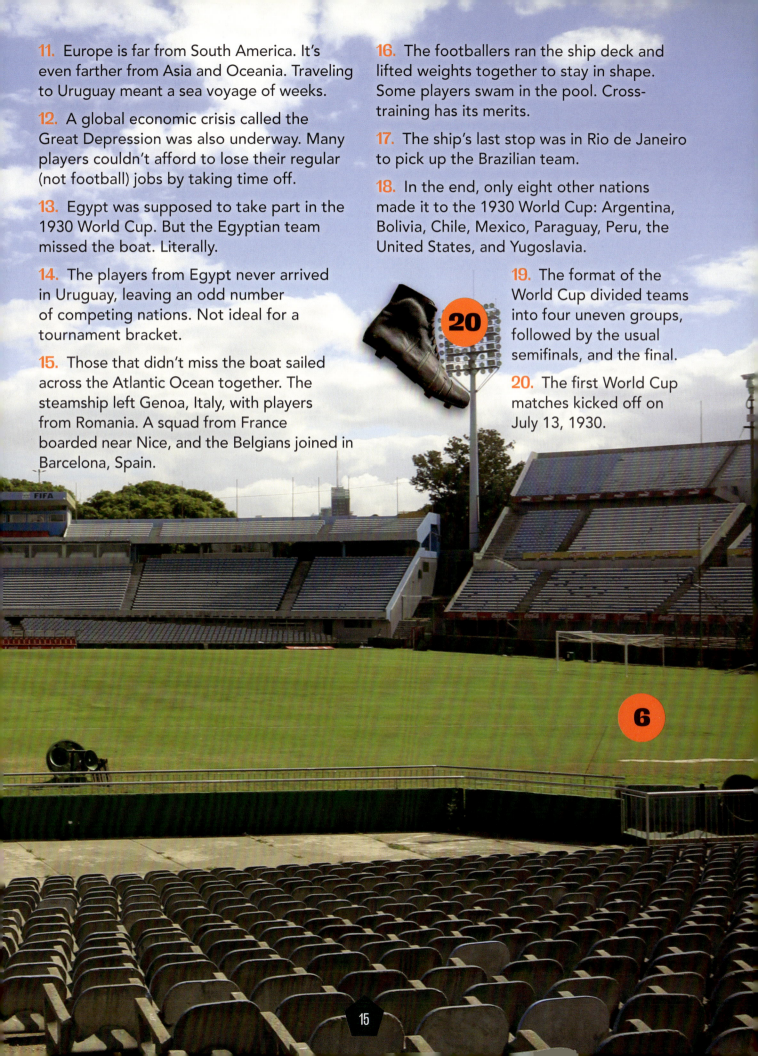

11. Europe is far from South America. It's even farther from Asia and Oceania. Traveling to Uruguay meant a sea voyage of weeks.

12. A global economic crisis called the Great Depression was also underway. Many players couldn't afford to lose their regular (not football) jobs by taking time off.

13. Egypt was supposed to take part in the 1930 World Cup. But the Egyptian team missed the boat. Literally.

14. The players from Egypt never arrived in Uruguay, leaving an odd number of competing nations. Not ideal for a tournament bracket.

15. Those that didn't miss the boat sailed across the Atlantic Ocean together. The steamship left Genoa, Italy, with players from Romania. A squad from France boarded near Nice, and the Belgians joined in Barcelona, Spain.

16. The footballers ran the ship deck and lifted weights together to stay in shape. Some players swam in the pool. Cross-training has its merits.

17. The ship's last stop was in Rio de Janeiro to pick up the Brazilian team.

18. In the end, only eight other nations made it to the 1930 World Cup: Argentina, Bolivia, Chile, Mexico, Paraguay, Peru, the United States, and Yugoslavia.

19. The format of the World Cup divided teams into four uneven groups, followed by the usual semifinals, and the final.

20. The first World Cup matches kicked off on July 13, 1930.

21. That brand-new stadium wasn't finished yet. France and Mexico had to play on the local club field in Montevideo.

22. The first-ever World Cup goal was scored by Frenchman Lucien Laurent.

23. France defeated Mexico, 4–1, but it was the only game they won in the tournament.

24. Just 300 fans watched the match the following day between Romania and Peru. It remains the lowest World Cup attendance ever.

25. The first hat trick in World Cup history was scored by Guillermo Stábile of Argentina on July 19, 1930.

26. That record stood until 2006. Wait, why would it change 76 years later?

27. According to recent FIFA research, a goal credited to an American, Tom Florie, in a Paraguay match two days earlier should have been awarded to his teammate, Bert Patenaude.

28. Let's try that again: The first hat trick in World Cup history was scored by Bert Patenaude of the United States on July 17, 1930.

29. After group play, Argentina, Uruguay, Yugoslavia, and the United States advanced to the semifinal round.

30. The United States took on Argentina, while Yugoslavia squared off against Uruguay.

31. Both the United States and Yugoslavia lost 6–1. Ouch.

32. Today, you can buy an actual ticket stub from the U.S.-Argentina semifinal of the 1930 World Cup. If you happen to have about $6,000 lying around.

33. The third-place match between Yugoslavia and the United States was never played.

34. Some said Yugoslavia refused to play as a protest against poor refereeing in their loss to Uruguay.

35. Apparently, in that World Cup semifinal, a police officer on the sideline kicked a ball into play—and Uruguay scored. The ref didn't notice.

36. At any rate, the U.S. and Yugoslavia both received bronze medals from the first ever World Cup.

37. Yugoslavia had been favored to win against the United States.

38. But the official record says the U.S. won third place because of a better goal differential.

39. Goal differential means the total number of team goals scored minus those given up.

40. To this day, the U.S.'s third-place finish in 1930 remains its best men's World Cup result.

41. More than 90,000 fans packed the Estadio Centenario in Montevideo for the first-ever World Cup final.

42. Workers had finished the stadium, with tower, just under the wire (well, five days late).

43. The final match of the 1930 World Cup took place on July 30, 1930.

44. Captains José Nasazzi of Uruguay and Manuel Ferreira shook hands before kickoff.

45. Argentina and Uruguay couldn't agree on an official match ball for the final.

46. The two sides finally settled on using two different balls. But not at the same time.

47. They played the first half with an Argentine ball, then switched to Uruguay's ball for the rest of the game.

48. Also on the field was José Leandro Andrade, a talented footballer and the sport's first Black Olympian. Win or lose, this World Cup final would be his last match for Uruguay.

49. After the whistle, it took Uruguay's Pablo Dorado just 12 minutes to score.

50. The (Argentine) ball went through the legs of the Argentinian goalkeeper.

51. Carlos Peucelle equalized eight minutes later.

52. Guillermo Stábile of Argentina scored in the 37th minute.

53. If you're keeping track, it was 2–1, Argentina up at halftime.

54. But Uruguay charged back in the second half, with goals from Pedro Cea, Santos Iriarte, and—with just one minute on the clock—Hector Castro.

55. Hmm, maybe Uruguay's own soccer ball was their good luck charm.

56. Final score: 4–2, Uruguay.

57. The first-ever World Cup crowd went wild. The Press Association later reported "scenes exceeding in enthusiasm even those of an English cup final."

58. As for the British fans, few were even aware the first World Cup had taken place.

59. The FIFA president, Jules Rimet, presented the trophy to the host team.

60. The Uruguayan government declared the next day a national holiday in honor of the win. Each member of the Uruguay team was given a house.

61. England may have started association football in 1863, but soccer was now a global sport.

62. One hundred years later, in 2030, Uruguay, along with Argentina and Paraguay, hosts the opening matches of the 24th World Cup.

GAME CHANGER
Pelé

1. He was known around the world as Pelé, though no one quite knows how he got the nickname.

2. Young Edson Arantes do Nascimento picked up the game in his poor Brazilian neighborhood.

3. At the age of nine, after Brazil's 1950 World Cup loss, Pelé told his tearful father: "Don't worry. I'm going to win one World Cup for you."

4. As it turned out, he won three (1958, 1962, 1970).

5. Pelé scored two goals in the final for his first World Cup when he was only 17.

6. He loved *o jogo bonito* ("the beautiful game"), focusing on ball control, creative passing, and attacking play.

7. In his time, unofficially speaking, Pelé scored more than 1,000 beautiful goals off both feet and his head.

8. He retired in 1974 after winning 10 Brazilian league titles.

9. Pelé joined the New York Cosmos to promote soccer in the U.S. They won a North American Soccer League championship in 1977.

10. Pelé was the Athlete of the Century, officially recognized by the International Olympic Committee in 1999. He died in 2022.

15 FACTS ABOUT THE FIRST WOMEN'S FOOTBALL MATCH

1. The *Glasgow Herald* reported on the historic event in Edinburgh, Scotland.

2. "A rather novel football match took place … between teams of lady players representing England and Scotland." This is the first written record of a women's soccer match—though it probably wasn't the first ever.

3. The game was held on May 7, 1881, at the local men's club, Hibernian Park.

4. "Upwards of a thousand persons witnessed it."

5. "The young ladies' ages appeared to range from eighteen to four-and-twenty."

6. "The [**Scottish**] team wore blue jerseys, white [baggy pants, and] red stockings while their **English** sisters were dressed in blue and white jerseys [and] blue stockings."

7. Players had a "fair idea of the game."

8. "During the first half the [Scottish] team, playing against the wind, scored a goal, and in the second half they added another two, making a total of three goals against their opponents' nothing."

9. Lily St Clair netted that first goal. She was the first woman documented as scoring in a football match.

10. This *Glasgow Herald* newspaper mention is likely the earliest record of women playing association football.

11. One week later, the women played another game in Glasgow, Scotland.

12. That match drew 5,000 spectators. (It didn't go well. Play ended in the second half after the crowd stormed the pitch, forcing the team to take cover.)

13. Today, a plaque at the Hibernian Park site commemorates this historic first in women's football history.

14. Another historic first in women's football: a match in 1920 in Liverpool, England, that sold more than 50,000 tickets.

15. A year later, the Football Association banned women footballers from their fields. Playing soccer wasn't ladylike. The ban lasted in some form for 50 years.

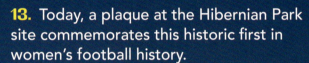

GAME CHANGERS
Nettie J. Honeyball and Lily Parr

1. Nettie J. Honeyball and **Lily Parr** were two of England's first women footballers.

2. Honeyball helped found the British Ladies Football Club. They played their first match in March 1895—North London versus South London.

3. The British Ladies Football Club players wore comfortable baggy pants called knickerbockers and shin pads.

4. The club held matches around the country, sometimes for as many as 10,000 ticket holders.

5. "I look forward to the time," **Honeyball** once said, "when ladies may sit in Parliament and have a voice in the direction of affairs, especially those which concern them most."

6. Lily Parr began playing in 1917 with the Dick, Kerr Ladies, a football team founded by an arms factory. She was 14.

7. In a story that might not be true, Parr once took a penalty kick that broke the goalkeeper's arm. That she scored 1,000 goals in her career is likely true.

8. One December afternoon in 1920, more than 50,000 fans paid to watch Parr's team defeat another club at Liverpool's Goodison Park.

9. It took 92 years for another women's football game to draw a larger crowd. That was at Wembley Stadium at the 2012 Olympics. (Great Britain beat Brazil.)

10. Despite the Football Association ban of women's football in 1921, Lily Parr played until 1951. She was inducted into England's National Football Hall of Fame in 2002, 24 years after her death.

THE STORY OF THE 1991 WOMEN'S WORLD CUP IN
50 PIVOTAL FACTS

1. The first-ever women's World Cup trophy was awarded 61 years after the first men's World Cup.

2. In the early 1970s, not many women's national teams were competing around the world.

3. There had been two international competitions in Italy and Mexico. Denmark won both.

4. Attendance at the finals of those women's competitions totaled 40,000 and 110,000.

5. In 1985, a small tournament called the Mundialito ("Little World Cup") was announced in Italy.

6. The United States had to scramble to assemble a women's national team. A coach selected 17 players, including college athletes Michelle Akers and Lori Henry.

7. "We wanted to be the best in the world," recalled Lori Henry years later, "even though there was no way to prove it."

8. The U.S. team had just three days to practice before flying to Europe.

9. On arrival, the women were each given $10 a day for food and an oversized men's kit with "USA" on the back.

10. How did the Americans do? Not well. They lost their first match against host Italy and finished last of the four teams.

11. In 1986, at the FIFA meeting in Mexico, a woman delegate from Norway stood to speak. She asked the FIFA president to promote women's football.

12. That Norwegian woman must have been compelling, as soon after, FIFA made an announcement.

13. FIFA would support a trial run—the FIFA International Women's Football Tournament in China in 1988.

14. Teams from 12 nations, including the United States and Canada, were invited.

15. More than 30,000 people watched Norway defeat Sweden, 1–0, in the final. (The United States had already lost to Norway in the quarterfinals.)

16. The 1988 event was successful enough to move ahead with the first-ever Women's World Cup, in 1991.

17. The 1991 event, however, was not considered an official World Cup and required funding from a candy company.

18. What was the name of the tournament back then? The First World Championship for Women's Football for the M&M's Cup.

19. Twelve nations qualified for the tournament: Brazil, China, Chinese Taipei, Denmark, Germany, Italy, Japan, New Zealand, Nigeria, Norway, Sweden, and the United States.

20. Sun Wen, an 18-year-old forward who later won the 1999 Golden Boot, played for China.

21. Anson Dorrance, a college soccer coach, had been hired in 1986 to lead the U.S. team.

22. Michelle Akers said, "Anson Dorrance had come in and said right away, 'We're going to be the best team in the world.' At the time we had no schedule, no support and there wasn't really any evidence to support Anson saying that. But we believed him."

23. Dorrance called up current and former college athletes to join the new squad. Only Akers and Henry were from the original 1985 national team.

24. Many of the others selected for the later renamed 1991 Women's World Cup would become legends of the sport.

25. The 1991 Women's World Cup squad included April Heinrichs, Carin Jennings, Joy Fawcett, Carla Overbeck, and Brandi Chastain. There were also three teenagers—Mia Hamm (9), Julie Foudy (11), and Kristine Lilly (13).

26. In planning for the tournament, FIFA had suggested using a smaller ball, an idea that was rejected.

27. All the women's matches lasted only 80 minutes. There was concern about whether they could play longer.

28. The 1991 Women's World Cup was the first and last time the women played less than the full 90 minutes.

29. For the first time in FIFA competition, six women served as match officials at the 1991 Women's World Cup. The third-place match was the first FIFA match ever officiated by a woman referee.

30. The United States steamrolled through group play, beating Sweden, Brazil, and Japan.

31. In the quarterfinals, the U.S. crushed Chinese Taipei, 7–0. Akers scored five of the seven goals.

32. During the tournament, the Chinese media dubbed Akers, Heinrichs, and Jennings "the Triple-Edged Sword." Playing as three attackers, they scored 20 of the team's 25 goals. Sharp!

33. According to Coach Dorrance, the U.S. had their own style of play: "We built our foundation on things like the individual duel. We were going to win every head ball, we were going to win every tackle, and we were going to win every one-v.-one contest."

34. The American style of play seemed to be working.

35. In the semifinals, the Americans beat Germany, 5–3. Jennings recorded a hat trick.

36. Silvia Neid, the 2007 World Cup-winning coach, played on the German team.

37. Then came the final: the U.S. versus Norway.

38. It had been a bumpy ride for the Norwegians, who lost the opening match in group play to China, 4–0.

39. "By the final game," U.S. coach Dorrance recalled later, "we were burned out. Absolutely knackered!"

40. On November 30, 1991, a crowd of 65,000 packed Tianhe Stadium in Guangdong, China.

41. Akers netted the first goal and Linda Medalen of Norway, the second. The score was even at halftime.

42. With three minutes remaining, Akers took advantage of a mistake by a Norwegian defender. She passed the goalkeeper and shot into the open goal.

43. The U.S. women had defeated Norway and earned their first World Cup trophy.

44. Michelle Akers finished as the tournament's top scorer, with 10 goals in six games.

45. The U.S. team's historic win was not widely covered back home. Only a few reporters and soccer officials greeted them at the airport.

46. "Nevertheless," Akers said, "our team pursued its vision. ... We focused on what we wanted the sport to become."

47. International TV crews had broadcasted highlights and full games to more than 100 nations.

48. More than half a million people attended the 1991 tournament of 12 nations.

49. The event was a sporting—and financial—triumph.

50. "Women's football is now well and truly established," FIFA's president said soon after.

GAME CHANGER
Michelle Akers

1. As a girl, Michelle Akers dreamed of being a Pittsburgh Steeler. For hours, she practiced catching that kind of football in her front yard in Seattle, Washington.

2. "I never felt like I lost out on things as a girl," said Akers. "At least not until the national team days, when you looked across at the men's team."

3. Akers attended the University of Central Florida on a soccer scholarship, winning NCAA All-American four times. She was the first woman to win the Hermann Trophy for college soccer.

4. In 1990, Akers became the first woman to sign a soccer brand endorsement—for Umbro.

5. She led the U.S. women to two World Cups (1991 and 1999) and an Olympic gold medal (1996).

6. Throughout, she dealt with illness, injury, and the challenges of being a pioneer.

7. "I play hard," she said, "and people just bounce off me or I go through them. I don't notice until after I get hit in the face."

8. In 1999, Akers appeared, arms raised in celebration, on the front of a Wheaties cereal box.

9. "She's the best woman that's ever played the game, period," U.S. women's coach Tony DiCicco said. "The way she heads passes. Her shot is incredibly hard with long-range accuracy. She can put a player onto the ball with 40-yard passes, right and left footed, and score a goal from 25 or 30 yards."

10. FIFA named Akers (and China's Sun Wen) best female player of the 20th century.

WHO RULES THE PITCH?

60 FACTS ABOUT **TROPHIES**, **STOLEN CUPS**, AND **A DOG NAMED PICKLES**

1. The first 1930 World Cup trophy was called *Victory*.

2. The trophy showed the goddess of victory in Greek mythology. Her name is Nike.

3. The small gold-plated silver statue rested on a base of blue stone called lapis lazuli.

4. After defeating Argentina in 1930, Uruguay kept the trophy until the next tournament.

5. The trophy traveled to Europe with the Italian team after their victory over Czechoslovakia in 1934. Italy kept the trophy for another four years after defeating Hungary in 1938.

6. During World War II, a FIFA official took the golden statue for safekeeping. Where did he put it? In a shoebox under his bed.

7. After the war, the trophy was renamed after Jules Rimet. He was the Frenchman who founded the tournament.

8. It was, after all, FIFA president Jules Rimet who lugged the trophy in his suitcase on the boat to Uruguay in 1930. Without him, there would have been nothing to award at the first World Cup.

9. The Jules Rimet Trophy was stolen in 1966. It was a few months before England was to host its first World Cup.

10. The trophy had been on display at a stamp exhibition in London.

11. No one knows for sure how the trophy was stolen, but the story involves poor security, a ransom note, and a failed swap.

12. In the end, a dog named Pickles discovered the stolen statue wrapped in newspaper under a bush in a park.

13. Police determined that the dog's owner was not involved in the robbery.

14. Pickles became a national hero, with his collar later displayed at the National Football Museum in Manchester. The border collie even appeared on a TV show. He was truly adorable.

15. About four months after police recovered the trophy, England won their first World Cup. The historic 1966 final took place at Wembley Stadium.

16. Queen Elizabeth awarded the recovered trophy to the English captain, Bobby Moore.

17. Before the 1930 World Cup, FIFA had agreed to award the trophy permanently to any nation that won three tournaments.

18. After their third win in 1970, Brazil took the Jules Rimet Trophy for keeps.

19. The third-time's-a-charm rule no longer applies for the World Cup, however. Germany, for instance, did not keep the trophy for their third win in 2014.

20. After 1970, the time had come to create a new World Cup.

21. More than 50 trophy designs from seven different countries were submitted.

22. The winning design came from Italy.

23. The trophy shows two human figures holding up Earth. Winning a World Cup may be just as hard.

24. The FIFA World Cup trophy is 14.4 inches (36.5 cm) tall.

25. It contains more than 13 pounds (6.2 kg) of gold that is 75 percent pure.

26. If the trophy were solid gold, it would weigh more than 150 pounds (68 kg).

27. The two bands around the trophy base are a green gemstone called malachite.

28. In 1970, it cost about $50,000 to make the trophy. Today, try $250,000.

29. Given its legacy, the World Cup might be the world's most valuable sports trophy.

30. Some say the World Cup is worth more than $20 million. Others say it's priceless.

31. Would you believe the Jules Rimet Trophy was stolen again in 1983? It was last seen in a bulletproof cabinet in the Brazilian Football Confederation in Rio de Janeiro.

32. FIFA has since made a replica of the Jules Rimet Trophy for display purposes.

33. The FIFA World Cup Trophy is usually kept at the FIFA Museum in Zurich, Switzerland.

Original Trophy

34. The trophy travels every four years to the tournament's host country, where it is awarded to the winning team. But they always give it back.

35. Don't worry: everyone who finishes first, second, or third at the World Cup goes home with a medal around their neck.

36. The winning team also gets to keep a gold-plate bronze replica of the World Cup. It is called the FIFA World Cup Winner's Trophy.

37. The only person to get a World Cup replica without winning a final—or any games for that matter—was Nelson Mandela.

38. The former president of South Africa was honored with a trophy for helping his country host the 2010 World Cup.

39. Not just anyone can touch the FIFA World Cup Trophy.

40. To touch the World Cup, you must be a member of the winning team, a head of state, a FIFA official, or a professional handler.

41. The name of every winning team since 1974 is engraved on the base of the FIFA World Cup.

42. When there's no more room, it will be time for a new FIFA World Cup design. Any ideas?

43. Today's FIFA Women's World Cup Trophy was created by a Lebanese designer from Milan, Italy.

44. The 10-pound (4.6 kg) trophy is a sleek spiral with a soccer ball at the top.

45. The statue, made of sterling silver, is covered in 23-karat white and yellow gold.

46. To quote FIFA, the Women's World Cup trophy symbolizes the "athleticism, dynamism, and elegance of women's football."

47. The trophy's platform shows the name of all the winning nations.

48. Like the men's trophy, the Women's World Cup trophy is awarded to the winning team immediately after the final.

49. The winning team takes home a replica called the FIFA Women's World Cup Winner's Trophy.

55

54. After the 2019 Women's World Cup, the trophy had a victory tour across the United States.

55. The trophy made 30 appearances, including in a televised New York City parade and at a National Football League game.

56. There was a different trophy for the first two Women's World Cups. It was a short statue of a soccer ball resting on a platform, and there were two copies.

57. Norway, after defeating Germany in 1995, took one trophy home—which has been stolen or lost since—and FIFA still has the other.

58. The men's and women's World Cup trophies sometimes leave Zurich, Switzerland, on tour.

59. The 2023 FIFA Women's World Cup Trophy tour traveled to the 32 participating nations to excite and inspire football fans.

60. FIFA aims to bring the FIFA World Cup Trophy to all of its members by 2030.

50. You can see the U.S. women's trophies from 1991, 1999, 2015, and 2019 at the National Soccer Hall of Fame in Frisco, Texas.

51. Even the FIFA Women's World Cup Winner's Trophies must be handled with special gloves to prevent damage.

52. When a winner's trophy goes on the road, extra security is required.

53. "These are really one-of-a-kind artifacts in U.S. soccer history," explained the director of the National Soccer Hall of Fame. "A person has to go with each and every one of them. They cannot be shipped at any point so they are on the airplane as carry-ons at all times."

THE EPIC 2022 MEN'S WORLD CUP FINAL IN
50 SHORT FACTS

1. The Argentina-France matchup in the 2022 World Cup final was nothing short of epic.

2. The 35-year-old Lionel Messi had appeared in four earlier World Cup tournaments but had yet to win a World Cup.

3. France's Kylian Mbappé was already defending a World Cup at just 23.

4. Messi, captain of his team, had scored in every match of the knockout stage.

5. Mbappé had scored five goals in the tournament, though not in the quarterfinal or semifinal.

6. An international crowd of some 89,000 fans filled the stadium in the coastal city of Lusail in Qatar.

7. For the first time ever, a World Cup final was being played in winter. But temperatures ranged from mild to hot in that part of the world.

8. On the west coast of the Persian Gulf, Qatar is mostly desert.

9. The ref's whistle blows, and play begins.

10. A penalty is called on French winger Ousmane Dembélé.

11. Dembélé has tripped Ángel Di María of Argentina in the box.

12. It is just 23 minutes into the match.

13. Lionel Messi steps up to take the kick.

14. Hugo Lloris, the French captain, is in goal.

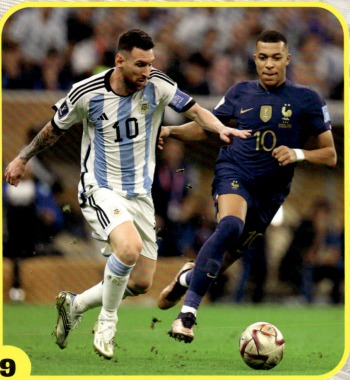

15. It is the two team captains facing off.

16. Messi takes his run-up to the ball and pauses slightly.

17. Then he slots it on the right past Lloris, who had lunged to the left.

18. 1–0 for Argentina. Messi takes a moment to celebrate.

19. Thirteen minutes later, Messi sets up a pass that leads to Di María lifting the ball over Lloris.

20. And it goes into the net, a second goal for Argentina, 2–0. Di María makes a heart sign, showing his love of the game.

21. Before the end of the first half, with France down by two, French stars Olivier Giroud and Ousmane Dembélé are subbed off.

22. In the second half, the score remains the same.

23. Now there's just twelve minutes to go in the game.

24. A penalty for France is called.

25. Mbappé steps up to take the kick and scores. Now it's 2–1.

26. Just 97 seconds later, Mbappé scores again. He takes a moment to celebrate. Now it's 2–2.

27. Regular time is over. Extra time is required.

28. Messi scores in the 108th minute.

29. Was Messi offside?

30. Everyone in the stadium is on their feet, looking to the referee.

31. No, it's a goal for Argentina, 3–2.

32. But then a French handball results in another nailed penalty kick for Mbappé, making the score 3–3.

33. Mbappé has scored a hat trick (the first in a men's World Cup final since Geoff Hurst's for England in 1966).

34. It's penalty shootout time.

35. Mbappé and Messi take—and make—the first penalties.

36. France shot, saved.

37. Argentina converts.

38. France misses the goal to the left.

39. Argentina scores, then France.

40. Gonzalo Montiel converts with a right-footed shot to the bottom left corner.

41. Players from the sideline stream onto the field.

42. Argentina triumphs in the 2022 World Cup, capturing their third title.

43. At long last, Lionel Messi has earned his own World Cup for Argentina.

44. The achievement sets his legacy as one of the three greatest footballers in history, alongside Pelé and the late Diego Maradona, also of Argentina.

45. Messi earns the 2022 Golden Ball for tournament's best player.

46. Emiliano Martínez wins the 2022 Golden Glove for best goalkeeping.

47. Mbappé takes the 2022 Golden Boot for most goals scored.

48. The 2022 Golden Boot winner is on the team that lost. It's a bit uncomfortable to walk by the trophy you lost as a team to accept one you won as an individual, but there you go.

49. Lionel Messi did the same when he accepted the 2014 Golden Ball after losing in the final to Germany.

50. This World Cup final ranks as one of the greatest. Epic, even.

GAME CHANGER
Diego Maradona

1. Diego Maradona was born in 1960 to a large, poor family outside of Buenos Aires, Argentina.

2. Diego got his first football at age three.

3. At age eight, Diego joined a soccer team called Las Cebollitas ("the Little Onions").

4. When he was 16, Diego became the youngest person to play on Argentina's national team.

5. He led his team to victory at the 1986 World Cup.

6. In the 1986 World Cup quarterfinal against England, Maradona punched the ball into the net with his hand. The referee mistook it for a header. Some later nicknamed it a "hand of God" goal. The ball sold at auction for nearly $2.4 million in 2022.

7. Maradona scored 259 goals in 490 official club games in his 21-year pro career.

8. He was named head coach of Argentina's national team in 2008.

9. In 2000, FIFA named Maradona the best player of the 20th century, alongside Pelé.

10. Diego Maradona, sometimes called El Pibe de Oro ("the Golden Boy"), died at age 60 in 2020.

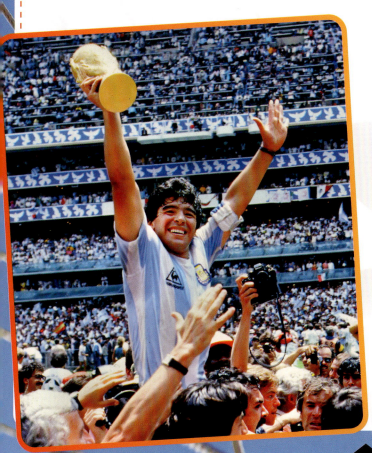

16 BEST FIFA MEN'S PLAYERS PAST AND PRESENT

This honor was known as the FIFA World Player of the Year from 1991 to 2009. It was called the FIFA Ballon d'Or from 2010 to 2015. Guess who has won it the most? Their name rhymes with "Bessie."

Player	Nation	Year(s) Won
Lionel Messi	Argentina	2009, 2010, 2011, 2012, 2015, 2019, 2022, 2023
Cristiano Ronaldo	Portugal	2008, 2013, 2014, 2016, 2017
Zinedine Zidane	France	1998, 2000, 2003
Ronaldo	Brazil	1996, 1997, 2002
Robert Lewandowski	Poland	2020, 2021
Ronaldinho	Brazil	2004, 2005
Vinícius Júnior	Brazil	2024
Luka Modric	Croatia	2018
Kaká	Brazil	2007
Fabio Cannavaro	Italy	2006
Luís Figo	Portugal	2001
Rivaldo	Brazil	1999
George Weah	Liberia	1995
Romário	Brazil	1994
Roberto Baggio	Italy	1993
Marco van Basten	Netherlands	1992
Lothar Matthäus	Germany	1991

GAME CHANGER
Lionel Messi

1. Young Lionel left Argentina to train in Spain with FC Barcelona. He was 13.

2. Messi is left-footed.

3. He stands 5 feet 7 inches (170 cm) tall.

4. After scoring, he often points at the sky with both hands.

5. It is a tribute to Messi's grandmother, who encouraged his love of soccer. She died when he was 11.

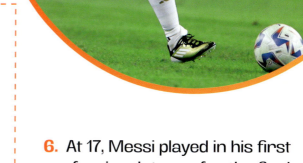

6. At 17, Messi played in his first professional game—for the final seven minutes.

7. A team's playmaker often wears the number 10. Messi inherited the number from Ronaldinho, his Barcelona teammate.

8. Messi became FC Barcelona's all-time leading goal scorer when he was only 24.

9. In 2022, he became the first player to win the World Cup's Golden Ball twice.

10. Many consider Messi the world's greatest soccer player. He has said, "When the day comes I'm not enjoying it, I will leave football."

22 NATIONS THAT HAVE LIFTED THE MEN'S WORLD CUP TROPHY

The first men's World Cup was held in 1930. Brazil holds the record for the most titles, though they haven't lifted the trophy since 2002.

Year	Winner	Final Opponent	Score	Host(s)
2022	Argentina	France	3–3 (4–2)*	Qatar
2018	France	Croatia	4–2	Russia
2014	Germany	Argentina	1–0**	Brazil
2010	Spain	Netherlands	1–0**	South Africa
2006	Italy	France	1–1 (5–3)*	Germany
2002	Brazil	Germany	2–0	Japan and South Korea
1998	France	Brazil	3–0	France
1994	Brazil	Italy	0–0 (3–2)*	U.S.
1990	West Germany	Argentina	1–0	Italy
1986	Argentina	West Germany	3–2	Mexico
1982	Italy	West Germany	3–1	Spain
1978	Argentina	Netherlands	3–1**	Argentina
1974	West Germany	Netherlands	2–1	West Germany
1970	Brazil	Italy	4–1	Mexico
1966	England	West Germany	4–2**	England
1962	Brazil	Czechoslovakia	3–1	Chile
1958	Brazil	Sweden	5–2	Sweden
1954	West Germany	Hungary	3–2	Switzerland
1950	Uruguay	Brazil	2–1	Brazil
1938	Italy	Hungary	4–2	France
1934	Italy	Czechoslovakia	2–1**	Italy
1930	Uruguay	Argentina	4–2	Uruguay

* = Match decided in penalty kicks (shootout score in parentheses).

** = Match decided in extra time.

9 NATIONS THAT HAVE LIFTED THE WOMEN'S WORLD CUP TROPHY

The first Women's World Cup tournament took place in 1991. The U.S. has won the Women's World Cup four times.

Year	Winner	Final Opponent	Score	Host(s)
2023	Spain	England	1–0	Australia and New Zealand
2019	U.S.	Netherlands	2–0	France
2015	U.S.	Japan	5–2	Canada
2011	Japan	U.S.	2–2 (3–1)*	Germany
2007	Germany	Brazil	2–0	China
2003	Germany	Sweden	2–1**	U.S.
1999	U.S.	China	0–0 (5–4)*	U.S.
1995	Norway	Germany	2–0	Sweden
1991	U.S.	Norway	2–1	China

* = Match decided in penalty kicks (shootout score in parentheses).

** = Match decided in extra time.

45 QUICK FACTS ABOUT THE ASTOUNDING 2015 WOMEN'S WORLD CUP FINAL
(ESPECIALLY THE FIRST 16 MINUTES)

1. BC Place in Vancouver, British Columbia, was packed, a sea of U.S. soccer T-shirts and American flags.

2. More than 53,000 fans took their seats in the stands. Millions more were watching from home.

3. The stage was set for the final of the 2015 Women's World Cup.

4. The U.S. lineup was unchanged from the semifinal victory over Germany.

5. U.S. star Carli Lloyd had scored in the three previous games.

6. Today, she wore the captain's armband.

7. The Japanese lineup was the same as their semifinal against England.

8. Today was a rematch of the 2011 World Cup final, which Japan won on penalties, but then the U.S. won gold when they met at the 2012 Olympics.

9. On the field today were 14 players—eight from Japan and six from the U.S.—who had started in the 2011 World Cup final.

10. Ayumi Kaihori and Hope Solo were once again in goal.

11. Expectations were high for an excellent battle.

12. The opening whistle blows, and play begins.

13. After just two minutes, the U.S. wins a corner kick.

14. Winger Megan Rapinoe takes it, delivering a low ball that skims the grass into the penalty area.

15. Lloyd is running. The left side of her foot makes contact with the ball, driving it in low for a goal.

16. After just 2 minutes, 34 seconds, Carli Lloyd has scored.

17. She has broken a record for the fastest goal in a Women's World Cup final.

18. Then, a free kick from midfielder Lauren Holiday sends a low ball into the box.

19. It's a jumping Lloyd who reaches it, tapping it into the goal with her right foot.

20. The game clock is at just 5 minutes.

21. Carli Lloyd has scored twice in about 135 seconds.

22. Then, with a strike off a flawed header from a defender, Holiday makes it 3–0.

23. The clock is at 14 minutes.

24. The Japan team huddles on the field for the third time, seemingly to regroup.

25. Two minutes later, Lloyd takes advantage of another mistake from Japan.

26. Boldly, Lloyd launches a long ball from midfield.

27. Her long-range effort travels 54 yards (49 meters).

28. The ball sails over the goalkeeper, who is caught far off her line, and into the net.

29. Reporters later call it "one of the most remarkable goals ever witnessed in a Women's World Cup."

30. Carli Lloyd has won a hat trick—the fastest in World Cup history, for men or women.

31. She is also the first American since Michelle Akers in 1991 to score more than one goal in a World Cup final.

32. It's 16 minutes since play began.

33. The score is 4–0.

34. Japan finally gets on the scoreboard in the 27th minute.

35. Early in the second half, the ball is deflected by midfielder Julie Johnston (now Ertz) into the U.S. net. It's an own goal, and it offers some hope for Japan.

36. The score is 4–2.

37. But two minutes later, Tobin Heath scores off of a corner kick.

38. Abby Wambach hits the field for her final World Cup appearance.

41

39. The referee blows the final whistle.

40. Score: 5–2.

41. The U.S. has won a record-breaking third World Cup, earning them a coveted third star, one for each victory.

42. Hope Solo takes the Golden Glove for best goalkeeping, allowing only three goals in the entire tournament.

43. Célia Sasic of Germany wins the Golden Boot for most tournament goals.

44. Carli Lloyd is awarded the Golden Ball for best player.

45. "I visualized playing in a World Cup final and scoring four goals," said Lloyd after the game. "It sounds pretty funny, but that's what it's all about. At the end of the day, you can be physically strong, you can have all the tools out there, but if your mental state isn't good enough, you can't bring yourself to bigger and better things."

44

GAME CHANGER
Emma Hayes

1. Emma Hayes was born in London, England, in 1976.

2. She played as a midfielder on an academy team for eight years.

3. When she was 17, Hayes hurt her ankle on a ski trip. The injury ended her soccer-playing career.

4. Unable to play, Hayes decided to pursue coaching, while she was in college.

5. With a one-way ticket and $1,000, she came to the United States to teach in youth soccer camps.

6. Hayes coached the Chicago Red Stars in the National Women's Soccer League for two years.

7. Hayes made a name for herself back in England at Chelsea FC Women, winning 16 trophies in 12 years.

8. Her motto? "Forget perfection, embrace your flaws, and be your best."

9. In just 10 matches, Hayes coached the U.S. women's national team to a gold medal at the 2024 Paris Olympics.

10. Emma Hayes was named the Best FIFA Women's Coach of the Year for 2024. She also received the first-ever *France Football*'s Ballon d'Or Women's Soccer Coach of the Year.

12 BEST FIFA WOMEN'S PLAYERS PAST AND PRESENT

This honor was first given to women in 2006. It was known as the FIFA Women's World Player of the Year until 2015. Before that, only men won the FIFA World Player of the Year. Who was the first winner? A hint: she goes by her first name.

Player	Nation	Year(s) Won
Marta	Brazil	2006, 2007, 2008, 2009, 2010, 2018
Birgit Prinz	Germany	2003, 2004, 2005
Alexia Putellas	Spain	2021, 2022
Carli Lloyd	U.S.	2015, 2016
Nadine Angerer	Germany	2013, 2014
Mia Hamm	U.S.	2001, 2002
Aitana Bonmatí	Spain	2023, 2024
Lucy Bronze	England	2020
Megan Rapinoe	U.S.	2019
Lieke Martens	Netherlands	2017
Abby Wambach	U.S.	2012
Homare Sawa	Japan	2011

GAME CHANGER
Marta

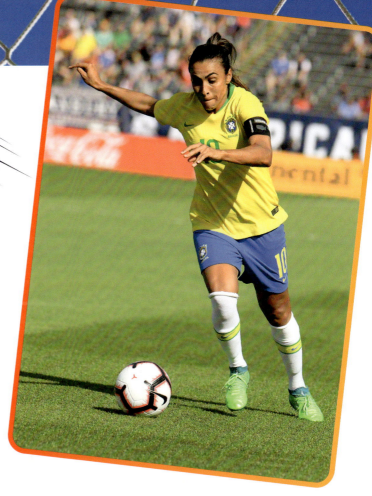

1. Marta Vieira da Silva goes by her first name. That's what most Brazilian players do.

2. She was born in 1986.

3. It was against the law in Brazil for women to play pro soccer until 1979.

4. As a child, Marta played soccer in the streets of her town.

5. "Believe in yourself," Marta told her fans, "and trust yourself because if you don't believe in yourself, no one else will."

6. Marta became the first soccer player to score a goal in five Olympics in a row in 2021.

7. Marta holds the record for most World Cup goals in history—17.

8. But the women's national team of Brazil has never won a World Cup.

9. Everyone agrees Marta is one of the game's best.

10. She announced her retirement from international play in 2024.

WHAT ARE THE RULES ANYWAY?

30 VERY SERIOUS FACTS ABOUT SOCCER BALLS

1. Youth soccer balls today come in five sizes, depending on the age of the player.

2. According to Law 2 of the official rules, international match balls must be round and of "suitable material."

3. At the start of a match, an official soccer ball must meet specific requirements for weight, size, and internal air pressure.

4. An official soccer ball must weigh between 14.5 to 16 ounces (410 to 450 grams).

5. An official soccer ball must measure 27 to 27.5 inches (68 to 70 cm) around.

6. An official soccer ball must have 0.6 and 1.1 atmospheres of air pressure.

7. The oldest soccer ball in the world is more than 450 years old. It doesn't meet FIFA regulations.

8. The world's oldest soccer ball is crafted from leather panels. Inside is a pig's bladder that requires inflating.

9. Workers in the late 1970s discovered the melon-sized ball behind roof panels in Scotland's Stirling Castle. This ball dates back to when Mary, Queen of Scots, lived there. Could the ball have been hers?

10. Early footballs were never completely round and rarely the same.

11. Early footballs could be hard to kick, pass, shoot—or catch.

12. Heading an early soccer ball's thick leather laces was difficult (and painful).

13. American Charles Goodyear introduced the first rubber soccer ball in 1855. It was a boxy ball with strong yet flexible (vulcanized) rubber panels, glued at the seams.

14. In 1863, Goodyear's ball was used in a match on Boston Common, organized by the first U.S. football club. The game combined soccer and rugby.

15. An English shoemaker created a rubber lining for leather footballs in 1862.

16. That same English shoemaker created a ball pump. You still had to stop during games to reinflate the ball. But no more blowing up animal bladders with your mouth.

17. You might know that James Naismith invented basketball in Springfield, Massachusetts, in 1891. Did you know it was first played with a soccer ball?

18. White soccer balls rolled in at the beginning of the 20th century.

19. White soccer balls were easier to see on grassy or muddy pitches.

20. Players appreciated that the white paint waterproofed the balls a bit. Untreated leather soaks up rain, and heavy soccer balls are not fun to kick or head.

21. White became a standard ball color for professional footballers in 1951.

22. Plastic balls often replaced leather ones in the 1960s. They were cheaper to make.

23. Adidas produced the first official World Cup ball in 1970. It was called the Telstar.

24. Made of 32 separate leather panels, the Telstar was the roundest soccer ball of the time.

25. The Telstar had 20 white six-sided shapes (hexagons) and 12 black five-sided shapes (pentagons).

26. A shape with 32 "faces" is called a truncated icosahedron (EYE-koh-suh-HEE-druhn).

27. Designers created the black-and-white Telstar to make the ball easier to see on television. (The World Cup was broadcast globally for the first time in 1970.)

28. Traditional soccer balls remain black and white.

29. The first non-leather World Cup match ball, the Azteca, was introduced in 1986.

30. Every FIFA World Cup ball since 1986 has been synthetic.

30 VERY IMPORTANT FACTS ABOUT SHIRTS, SOCKS, AND SHIN GUARDS

1. All soccer players must wear proper equipment on the field.

2. Proper soccer equipment means a shirt with sleeves, shorts, socks, and footwear.

3. The word *cleat* does not appear in FIFA's official rules.

4. A shin guard is worn to help protect a soccer player's shin from injury.

5. All soccer players must wear shin guards underneath the socks.

6. Soccer referees regularly do shin guard inspections. Are they the right size for the player?

7. Shin guards should be no more than 2 inches (5 cm) above the ankle.

8. There is nothing in the FIFA rules that says what size a shin guard must be.

9. Some people think the trend of wearing "micro" or "mini" shin pads is unsafe. Jack Grealish of England wears them all the time, however.

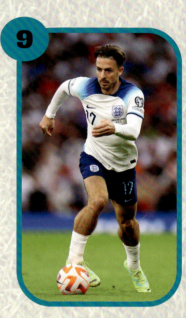

10. Spoiler alert: Getting kicked in the shin, where there is no muscle or fat protecting the bone, really hurts.

11. Greek and Roman warriors benefited from leg protection during battle.

12. The earliest shin guards are from 700 BCE.

13. Athletes first used shin guards during cricket.

14. In the late 19th century, English cricketer/footballer Sam Weller Widdowson had an idea to prevent injury in chippy football games. (*Chippy* means "rough or physical.")

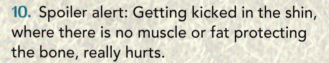

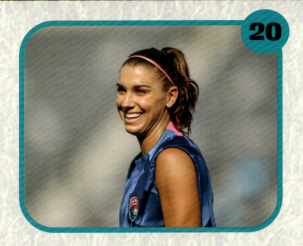

15. Widdowson, in 1874, cut down his large cricket pads and strapped them over his socks. Other players laughed at him, but minds were changed, and the rest is history.

16. FIFA has required players to wear shin guards since 1990.

17. Some pro athletes play with custom shin guards, with pictures of family or pets on them. Whatever works.

18. You may use pre-wrap around your shins, but it must be underneath the guards. (Pre-wrap is used under athletic tape to protect the skin.)

19. You can use pre-wrap as headwear. Plenty of footballers use both rolled and flat styles.

20. Alex Morgan popularized the use of pink pre-wrap. When she was young, it helped her family find her on the playing field.

21. If your boot or shin guard comes off, you must put it back on when the ball goes out of play, or earlier if possible.

22. If you happen to score without your boot or shin guard before you can put it back on, the goal counts.

23. No "dangerous jewelry" is permitted on the pitch.

24. Perhaps it's obvious, but footballers on the same team must wear the same color uniform. (The goalkeeper wears a different color.)

25. The visiting team wears solid white jerseys and socks.

26. The home team wears jerseys and socks that are dark or any color that contrasts with white.

27. Nouhaila Benzina of Morocco became the first soccer player to wear a hijab—a head covering worn by some Muslim women—at a World Cup match in 2023. It was not permitted before 2014.

28. At the World Cup, each team has an official kit and a reserve kit.

29. The rules say teams should wear their official kit unless the colors are too similar.

30. In that case, one team wears its reserve kit.

25 VERY OFFICIAL FOOTBALL TERMS

1. A **challenge** is when a player competes with an opponent for the ball.

2. **Charging** means physically challenging an opponent for the ball, usually by using the shoulder and upper arm with the arm close to the body.

3. To protect player safety, **cooling breaks** are allowed in high heat and humidity to help lower body temperatures. They typically last 90 seconds to 3 minutes.

4. The first World Cup cooling break took place in 2014 after temperatures hit 102 degrees Fahrenheit (39 degrees Celsius) inside the stadium in Brazil. Players got three minutes to rest and rehydrate.

5. **Electronic performance and tracking systems (EPTS)** track information about a player's physical performance. They analyze heart rate, muscle activity, position, speed, and distance covered in a match. Foot-worn devices are now permitted in official FIFA games.

6. **Excessive force** is using more strength than is necessary on the pitch.

7. **Feinting** is a move meant to confuse your opponent. Deceptive or distracting moves are allowed during open play or when taking a free kick. (Feinting is not permitted after the run-up for a penalty kick.)

8. The **field of play** is the playing area, as marked by the goal lines and the sidelines, or touchlines.

9. A **friendly** is a match between two national teams that has no impact on league or championship play. (It can affect FIFA world rankings, however.)

10. **Goal Line Technology (GLT)** is an electronic system that notifies the referee when the ball has fully crossed the goal line.

11. A **holding offense** happens when a player's contact with an opponent or their equipment keeps the opponent from moving.

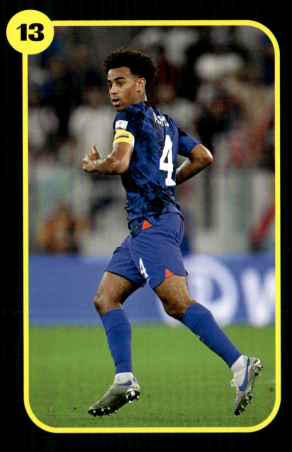

12. A **match report** is the official record of a game, including disciplinary actions and any other incidents before, during, or after the match.

13. A **national team captain**, chosen by the head coach, leads the team and performs the coin toss before kickoff. A trial FIFA rule says only the captain can approach the referee over calls. U.S. midfielder Tyler Adams, at 23, was the youngest 2022 World Cup captain.

14. **Reckless plays** are any action, usually a tackle or challenge, by a player that disregards the danger to the opponent.

15. The team **roster** is the official list of the players eligible to play in a game.

16. Punishment from the referee is called a **sanction**.

17. **Serious foul play** is a tackle or challenge for the ball that endangers an opponent's safety or uses excessive force.

18. **Simulation** is when a player pretends something happened on the pitch to gain an unfair advantage.

19. The **starting lineup** is the official list of players who will start a game.

20. **Suspending a match** is stopping play for a period of time due to something such as bad weather or a serious injury.

21. A **team list** is the official team document of players, substitutes, and team officials.

22. Team officials, or **technical staff**, are any non-players listed on the official team list, such as coaches, physical therapists, or doctors.

23. **Unsporting behavior** is an unfair action or behavior. It can earn a caution.

24. A **VAR (Video Assistant Referee) review** allows officials to use video technology to check key incidents and help the referee make calls.

25. VAR was used for the first time in a World Cup final in 2018 to award France a penalty for an Ivan Perisic (4) handball. Croatia lost, 4–2.

36 COLORFUL FACTS ABOUT CARDS

3

1. Who invented red and yellow cards in soccer? English referee Ken Aston introduced them during the 1970 World Cup in Mexico.

2. Aston said the idea of colored cards came to him while stopped at a traffic light.

3. "The traffic light turned red," Aston explained later. "I thought, 'Yellow, take it easy; red, stop, you're off.'"

4. Fouls abound in soccer.

5. For a basic foul, the referee stops play and awards a free kick. Basic fouls are given for careless plays.

6. For more dangerous plays, out come the cards.

7. A yellow card is a referee's official caution to a player.

8. A red card is for the worst offenses. Red means a player is ejected from the game. (And not playing in the next game either.)

9. Most red cards are for excessive force during a play.

10. Two yellows in one match result in an immediate red card.

11. Referees issue yellows mostly for "reckless" plays.

12. They also issue yellows for fouls that interfere with or stop a promising attack.

13. Two yellow cards over two games take you out of the next game.

14. A World Cup referee in a 2022 quarterfinal once handed out 18 yellow cards.

15. Lionel Messi wasn't pleased, later calling the ref not "up to the task." Argentina beat Netherlands anyway.

16. You can get a yellow card for arguing with the referee. No one likes disrespect.

17. You can get a yellow card for removing your jersey during a goal celebration. No one likes a show-off.

18. Taking too long for a throw-in (to run out the remaining time) can mean a yellow card.

19. Pretending to be hurt (to win a foul) can mean a yellow card.

20. A red card requires a player to leave the field right away. No standing on the sideline.

21. After a red card, the team must play with just 10 players for the rest of the match.

22. Rachel Buehler received her first-ever red card in the 2011 Women's World Cup quarterfinals. ("I don't really even get yellow cards," the U.S. defender said after.) She was blocking Brazil's Marta.

23. A red card for the defending team inside the box results in a penalty kick for the other side. If they convert—like Marta did after Buehler's red card in the box—that's a kick that hurts.

24. Playing a (wo)man down, the U.S. team went on to beat Brazil in a penalty shootout. Phew.

25. Even a goalkeeper can get a red card.

26. If there are no more subs when a goalkeeper gets a red card, a field player must take their place. Fingers crossed on that one.

27. Referees often put the red card and the yellow card in different pockets. That way, they won't pull out the wrong one by accident.

28. The referee shows a player a card and writes the name in a notebook.

29. That's why it's called a "booking."

30. There has been talk of a blue card. It would bench a player for 10 minutes for offenses worse than yellow but not quite a red. So no talking back to the ref.

31. Oh, for talking back to the ref, a coach can also be red-carded.

32. How many red cards is too many for a team? More than four. (A team must have seven players on the field to participate.)

33. Did you know that spitting at someone can get you a red card?

34. In the 2006 World Cup final, France's Zinedine Zidane headbutted a player from Italy.

35. He collected a red card.

36. France ended up losing 5–3 on penalties. "I'm not at all proud of what I did, but it's part of my past," Zidane said later of his last-ever game.

GAME CHANGER
Zinedine Zidane

1. This attacking midfielder is famous for the Zidane pirouette. It's a spin turn to move the ball around a defender.

2. Zidane scored 31 goals in 108 games for France. Two were in the 1998 World Cup final, which France won.

3. Even with a red card in the 2006 World Cup final, Zidane won the Golden Ball as the tournament's best player.

4. Lionel Messi has said of trading jerseys at the end of games: "I am not one to ask to swap shirts. I asked once … I asked Zidane."

5. Zinedine Zidane was born in Marseilles, France, to Algerian parents.

6. He faced racism growing up.

7. Zinedine is an Arabic name that means "the beauty of faith."

8. "Often young players are taught to shoot like this, pass like that," Zidane once said. "Today the kids between eight and ten should play for fun."

9. Zidane managed Real Madrid after his playing career. They won a record three Champions League titles in a row. He left in 2021.

10. It was Zidane who passed the Olympic torch to Spanish tennis great Rafael Nadal in the 2024 opening ceremony in Paris.

30 KICKIN' FACTS

1. All soccer games start with a **kickoff**.

2. Before the kickoff, the referee tosses a coin, and the visiting team captain calls heads or tails.

3. The winner of the coin toss gets to choose the kickoff or the side of the field to attack for the first half. The loser of the coin toss gets whatever the winner didn't choose—the side of the field to attack for the first half or the kickoff.

4. A kickoff starts the second half of a soccer game too.

5. The team that didn't take the kickoff to start the first half takes the kickoff to start the second half.

6. A kickoff starts both halves of extra time in a soccer game.

7. A kickoff also restarts play after a goal.

8. For a kickoff, the ball goes on the center mark—the middle of the halfway line and the center of the circle.

9. Opponents must be at least 10 yards (9 meters) away from the ball during a kickoff.

10. After the ref blows the whistle, the soccer ball is in play when it is kicked and clearly moves.

11. A **direct kick** is a free kick awarded by the referee that allows a player to score directly.

12. An **indirect kick** is a free kick awarded by the referee that requires a player to pass the ball to another player before a goal can be scored.

19

13. By the way, a player cannot score directly from a throw-in. The ball must touch another player before a goal can be scored.

14. Any player, including the goalkeeper, may take a goal kick.

15. A **goal kick** restarts play after the attacking team sends the entire ball over the goal line. (Except if it's a goal. Then, there is a kickoff. See above.)

16. A **corner kick** restarts play after the ball goes over the goal line, last touched by a defensive player.

17. Cesáreo Onzari of Argentina scored against Uruguay from a corner kick at the 1924 Olympics. There was some confusion about whether scoring from a corner kick was permitted. It was.

18. Scoring directly from a corner kick is now known as *gol olímpico* (Spanish for "Olympic goal").

19. U.S. star Megan Rapinoe is the only footballer to score two olímpicos at the Olympics (in 2012 and 2020).

20. Argentina superstar Lionel Messi, even after more than 800 career goals, hasn't ever scored one directly from a corner kick.

21. A **volley kick** is a kick of the soccer ball before it rebounds or touches the ground.

22. A **bicycle kick** is an example of a volley kick. It's sometimes called an overhead kick or a scissor kick.

23. To do a bicycle kick, the player somersaults backward. At the same time, they move their legs in a pedaling motion and strike the ball in the air.

24. A bicycle kick is as impressive looking as it sounds, especially if the ball ends up in the net.

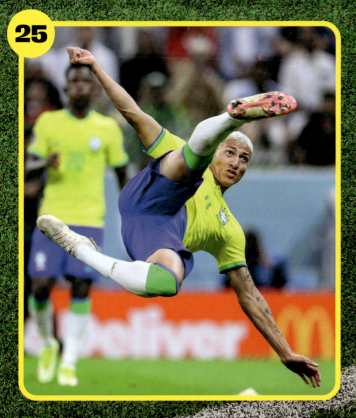

25. Many called Richarlison's stunning bicycle kick—which sent the ball into the net in Brazil's game against Serbia—the 2022 World Cup's best goal.

26. A **toe poke** is a kick made with the end of the toe. Foot doctors don't recommend it.

27. A **backheel** is a kick of the ball with the heel.

28. A **penalty kick** is a direct free kick taken about 12 yards (11 meters) in front of the center of the goal.

29. A penalty kick is awarded when a player from the opposing team commits a foul inside their own penalty area.

30. At the 2023 Women's World Cup, Chloe Kelly scored the game-winning penalty kick against Nigeria, sending England into the quarterfinals. Her kick was clocked at 68.8 miles (110.7 km) per hour. That's faster than the speed limit on many highways.

12 EXCELLENT QUESTIONS
ABOUT OFFSIDES, THE CLOCK, AND PKs

1. What is "offside" anyway?

Put simply: A player is offside when they go behind the line of opposing defenders before the ball has been kicked to them. Put less simply: The attacking player must be in the opponents' half of the field. They must be closer to the goal line than any defender. They must be actively involved in the play. The offside rule keeps players from just waiting around by the goal to score.

2. What is the difference between regulation time, full time, and regular time?

Nothing. Regulation time, full time, and regular time are the normal length of the game before extra time is added. In other words, it's 90 minutes plus any stoppage time.

3. What is the difference between stoppage time, injury time, added time, and additional time?

Nothing. Stoppage time, injury time, added time, and additional time are terms for the same thing. They are the minutes that referees add to the game clock after 90 minutes. Those minutes make up for time lost to goal celebrations, substitutions, the awarding of cards, video review, and treating injuries.

1

4. How is stoppage time decided? How do the players find out?

The referee keeps track of all pauses in play during the game. After adding that up, the referee communicates the total minutes to the match official on the sideline. That person then holds up the number on the electronic board for everyone to see.

5. What about extra time?

Extra time is not the same as stoppage time. If a game is tied after 90 minutes plus stoppage time, the game goes into extra time. Teams play another 30 minutes—two halves of 15 minutes each—to see if they can win.

6. Can there be stoppage time after extra time?

Yes.

7. What happens when a player puts the ball in their own net?

It's called an own goal, and it counts. It's a fortunate break for the other side. But it can also inspire the team to recover quickly by scoring again—in the right net.

8. How do they do penalty shootouts again?

A coin toss decides which team takes the first penalty kick (PK) in a shootout. Each team takes five penalties in alternating turns. No player may take more than one. If one team has a lead that the other team cannot overcome, the shootout—and the game—is over. If the score is tied after 10 penalties, the winner is the side that scores when the opposing side misses.

9. Why do teams usually choose to take the first kick in a penalty shootout?

Choosing to go first seems to increase a team's chance of success. One report says about 60 percent of the teams that took the first kick ended up winning the game.

10. Is it harder for the goalkeeper to save a penalty kick or the taker to score one?

The odds are stacked against the goalkeeper. With only a split-second to react, goalkeepers have to defend the entire goal. The ball comes fast from fairly close range. Penalty takers have time to aim for spots that are difficult to reach. Nailing the penalty kick is cause for celebration. But saving a penalty kick is considered one of the most impressive achievements in soccer. It can be the difference between winning and losing the game.

10

11. When someone misses a PK, is the next person more likely to miss?

According to experts, penalty takers score about 85 percent of the time during regular play. However, during a penalty shootout, that number falls to about 75 percent. The pressure of knowing that their kick could decide the game is likely to affect players' performance.

12. Are there any strategies for taking a PK?

Penalty takers try to stay calm. They need to manage their stress. They often picture in advance their shot sailing over the goal line and hitting the back of the net. They avoid focusing on the goalkeeper. They usually decide on a spot to aim for and stick with it. They pause after the referee's whistle before their run-up, then hit their spot.

GAME CHANGER
Christian Pulisic

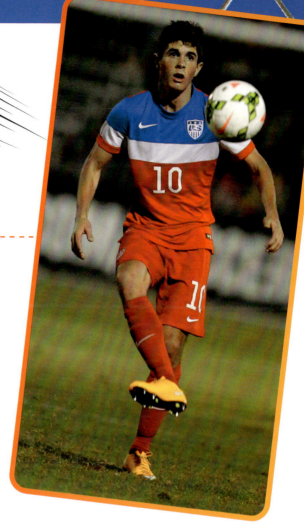

1. Christian Pulisic was born in 1998 in Hershey, Pennsylvania, to parents who both played soccer in college.

2. When he was young, Christian lived near Oxford, England, for a year with his family. He attended many Tottenham Hotspur and Manchester United games.

3. Pulisic has Croatian nationality, but he chose to play soccer for the United States national team.

4. The midfielder earned his first cap for the U.S. men's national team at age 17.

5. Pulisic earned five goals in his first full season with the German club team Borussia Dortmund. He was only 18 years old.

6. At age 20, in 2018, Pulisic became the youngest captain in the modern history of the men's U.S. national team.

7. Christian Pulisic scored his 10th international goal in 2019, making him the youngest American man to achieve that feat.

8. In 2021, Pulisic became the first American to score in a men's Champions League semifinal, for Chelsea against Real Madrid.

9. Pulisic was the first American to play in and then win a men's Champions League final, also in 2021. (Chelsea beat Manchester City, 1–0).

10. Pulisic's leadership, along with his speed, dribbling, and finishing, have earned him the nickname Captain America.

30 FACTS ABOUT GOALKEEPERS (AND SCORING ON THEM)

1. Goalkeepers are allowed to wear (big) gloves.

2. The goalkeeper has to defend a goal 24 feet (7.3 meters) wide and 8 feet (2.4 meters) tall.

3. Technically, it's OK for a keeper to put substances on their gloves, such as petroleum jelly. Putting gel on keeper gloves might improve grip on the ball, but it may damage the gloves over time.

4. Goalkeepers must wear colors that are different from the other players and the match officials.

5. If the two goalkeepers are wearing the same color and neither has another shirt, the game may begin anyway.

6. In international play, the kit maker selects the color of the keeper's uniform.

7. Goalkeepers often wear a bright color.

8. Studies suggest it may be harder for players to score on keepers in red or yellow.

9. Goalkeepers may wear athletic pants.

10. Goalkeepers may wear knee and arm protectors. Padding on your body helps when you're diving for balls.

11. Inside the penalty box, goalkeepers can use any part of their body, including their hands.

12. Outside the penalty box, goalkeepers are just like any other player.

13. Players may not challenge a goalkeeper holding the ball.

14. If a teammate kicks the ball back to the goalkeeper, the goalkeeper may not pick up the ball. They have to play it with their feet.

15. The back-pass violation was introduced in 1992 to prevent time wasting.

16. There's a certain amount of running down the clock when your team is ahead.

17. The six-second rule was introduced in 1998, also to prevent time wasting. After six seconds of holding the ball, a goalkeeper must play it.

30

18. The punishment for holding the ball too long is an indirect free kick at that spot for the opposing team.

19. Referees don't enforce the six-second rule often. It is pretty harsh: the other team might end up with a goal.

20. There is a proposed change to the six-second rule. Under a new rule, the referee would give a hand signal after five seconds. If the goalkeeper goes over eight seconds, the referee would award a throw-in or a corner kick.

21. A teammate may change places with the goalkeeper as long as it's during an official stop in play.

22. For a goal to count, the ball must cross the goal line between the posts completely.

23. If a keeper catches a ball behind the goal line between the posts, it still counts as a goal.

24. Saving (or trying to save) penalty kicks is a crucial job of a goalkeeper.

25. The goalkeeper must have a foot on the goal line until the penalty taker kicks the ball.

26. If the goalkeeper moves off the goal line before the ball is kicked, the penalty may be taken again.

27. Stutter steps in the run-up to a penalty kick are allowed. Remember? That's called feinting.

28. Penalty takers may not fake kick at the end of the run-up to the ball. That's called illegal feinting.

29. A goalkeeper may take penalty kicks.

30. In 2024, U.S. keeper Alyssa Naeher completed a "Naeher sandwich" during international play—saving a penalty kick, scoring one, and then saving another. She did it again in a different match. She retired later that year.

24 FACTS ABOUT REFEREES AND WHAT THEY DO

1. The referee has full authority to enforce the "laws" of the game. That includes stopping play, awarding free kicks, and issuing cards.

2. The referee acts as match timekeeper.

3. The referee oversees when and how play restarts on the field.

4. What does a referee need for every game? A whistle, a watch, cards (red and yellow), and a notebook or something similar to keep track of time and cautions.

5. Headsets are key for good communication on the pitch.

6. Referees and other on-field match officials may not wear jewelry on the job.

7. Referees may use fitness-monitoring equipment to track their physical performance during a game.

8. Referees must train physically, including sprints and interval running, to stay fit for the game. They must complete yo-yo tests, running between cones to assess agility, endurance, and strength.

9. The assistant referees signal when the ball is out of play and which team takes the corner kick, goal kick, or throw-in.

10. Assistant referees signal when players are offside and help oversee penalty kicks.

11. Assistant referees use buzzer or beep flags. A button on the flag triggers a vibration on the referee's armband to communicate offside calls during loud matches.

12. Closer offside calls require a Video Assistant Referee (VAR) review.

13. If a ref puts their finger to the ear and extends the other hand, it means "checking."

14. Making a big horizontal box with both arms indicates a VAR review. That's called the "TV signal."

15. The video match official helps the referee review replay footage for clear errors or serious missed incidents involving scoring, penalties, and red cards.

16. The assistant referee on the sideline holding that big electronic board is called the fourth official.

17. The fourth official manages substitutions, oversees replacement balls, and monitors behavior of team officials.

18. FIFA appointed 36 referees, 69 assistant referees, and 24 video match officials for the 2022 World Cup in Qatar.

19. FIFA appointed 33 referees, 55 assistant referees, and 19 video match officials for the 2023 Women's World Cup in Australia and New Zealand.

20. Sometimes players refuse to shake hands with referees at the end of matches. But that's not very sporting.

21. What happens if the ball hits a referee during play? If it leads to a promising attack or a possession change, play is stopped. The game then restarts with a drop ball.

22. French referee Stéphanie Frappart took charge of the 2019 Women's World Cup final. (The U.S. beat the Netherlands, 2–0.)

23. In 2022, Frappart became the first woman to referee a men's World Cup match. (Germany beat Costa Rica during the group stage, 4–2.)

24. Why do referees talk so much to the players in soccer? Referees communicate with players to maintain control of the game and ensure fair play. "When they're calm, not when you've just made a decision, but as part of a game, when you pass close to them—then I like to discuss the decision with them," Frappart explained. "Remember, most of the time, they are under pressure too."

LEAVING IT ALL ON THE FIELD

6 WAYS TO CELEBRATE A WORLD CUP GOAL

Fans love seeing how footballers respond after those unforgettable moments in front of the goal. World Cup goal celebrations can be as crazy as the goals themselves. How would you celebrate?

1. **Kylian Mbappé** folds his arms, tucking his hands underneath his armpits, after goals. That's his signature celebration. He's even trademarked it. While Mbappé and his younger brother were playing a game of *FIFA* on the PlayStation, his brother apparently crossed his arms in a pose after scoring.

"Five minutes later," explained Mbappé, "he stopped and said, 'Kylian, you could do that in a match.' So I did." Mbappé pulled out his goal celebration several times during the 2022 World Cup. In fact, he won the Golden Boot as the tournament's top scorer. Despite Mbappé's hat trick in the final, France lost to Argentina in a penalty shootout.

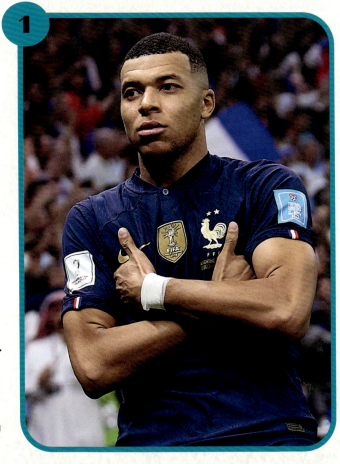

2. **José Roberto Gama de Oliveira**, known as Bebeto, scored more than 39 international goals for Brazil. His most famous was the second goal in the 1994 World Cup quarterfinal against the Netherlands. Bebeto seized a loose ball and raced past the Dutch goalkeeper to score. He then sprinted to the sideline and pretended to cradle a baby. Fellow players Romário and Mazinho ran to each side of him and did the same.

"It was spontaneous. Nothing had been planned. But I was pleasantly surprised to see some of my teammates joining me in celebrating that goal," Bebeto recalled. "At first, no one outside the team knew about our son being born. But later, I explained to the world." Brazil won the game and went on to beat Italy in the final. The new father, whose son had been born just two days before the game, played every minute of the tournament and scored three goals total.

3. One 1994 World Cup goal resulted in a quirky celebration. Nigeria was in its first-ever World Cup. When **Finidi George** scored against Greece, he dropped on all fours like a dog. He even lifted a back leg as if to pee. The goal was far more elegant—a chip over the goalkeeper.

"It's the World Cup and all eyes are on you. You score a goal and you just go crazy," George explained later. "That's what happened to me when I celebrated like that."

4. **James Rodríguez** of Colombia became a star at the 2014 World Cup, scoring six goals in just five matches. He earned the tournament's Golden Boot at just 22 years old. But James Rodríguez will be remembered as much for his salsa choke. After scoring a header off a corner kick against Côte d'Ivoire, he sprinted to the side. Rodríguez (10) led his teammates in a kind of hip-hop line dance, inspired by a fellow Colombian, singer Shakira. The crowd roared its approval.

"So many people rooting for you, it was extraordinary," said Rodríguez. "It was very loud, and it was in our favor so that Colombia could win." And they did win that game, 2–1, though Colombia was defeated by Brazil in the quarterfinals.

"As soon as the ball left my foot, I knew it was going in," **Siphiwe Tshabalala** recalled. "It was just a surreal moment. It took me back to when I was a kid, the joy I had when I played football. When I was a kid, I used to dream about scoring important goals. Whenever we would score, we would run around and celebrate while cheering for ourselves." Teammates ran over to the corner flag to join Tshabalala (8). They danced in unison, the stadium cheering them on.

5. After notching his first World Cup goal, the typically reserved **Clint Dempsey** broke out a quick stutter-step celebration. The 26-year-old Texan was the only U.S. player to find the back of the net at the 2006 World Cup. His goal came off a pass from DaMarcus Beasley just before halftime in the match against Ghana.

Dempsey still remembers the moment: "It's my favorite goal and my favorite memory in my football career. Being in a World Cup and scoring a goal, that's when I knew I had arrived, that I had made it. That's when I knew anything was possible."

6. "Goal for South Africa! Goal for all of Africa!" shouted the TV commentator. A South African had scored the opening goal of the 2010 World Cup in South Africa, the tournament's first African nation to host.

15 TOP MEN'S WORLD CUP "GOOOOOAL!" SCORERS

More than 2,700 goals have been scored at 22 men's World Cups. That total does not include penalty shootouts. Who has scored the most? And over how many matches?

Player	Nation	WC Matches	WC Goals
Miroslav Klose	Germany	24	16
Ronaldo	Brazil	19	15
Gerd Müller	West Germany	13	14
Just Fontaine	France	6	13
Lionel Messi	Argentina	26	13
Kylian Mbappé	France	14	12
Pelé	Brazil	14	12
Sándor Kocsis	Hungary	5	11
Jürgen Klinsmann	West Germany/Germany	17	11
Helmut Rahn	West Germany	10	10
Gabriel Batistuta	Argentina	12	10
Gary Lineker	England	12	10
Teófilo Cubillas	Peru	13	10
Thomas Müller	Germany	19	10
Grzegorz Lato	Poland	20	10

5 MORE WAYS TO CELEBRATE A WORLD CUP GOAL

Scoring in the World Cup is a moment every serious footballer dreams of. What they do afterward often reflects the emotion and meaning of the achievement. Other times, it's just silly.

1. It was one of the most electrifying moments—and celebrations—in soccer history. After stepping up and calmly slotting the winning penalty kick in the 1999 Women's World Cup final, **Brandi Chastain** ripped off her jersey in elation. The U.S. defender dropped to her knees, fists raised in the air with joy. An iconic photo of that moment later appeared on the cover of *Sports Illustrated*, capturing the raw emotion. Since then, Chastain has been often asked about her goal and celebration.

One answer she gave: "It was a combination of things: joy, relief, satisfaction, the desire to do well for your team, your country, your family—those are emotions that you carry around every day for years and finally I could let it all out."

2. **Alex Morgan** pretended to drink a cup of tea. She even curled her pinky finger. It happened after the American's goal against England in the semifinal of the 2019 Women's World Cup. Some thought she was mocking the English. Others wondered if she was referring to the Boston Tea Party. (That's when American colonists dumped tea in the harbor to protest British taxes in 1773.)

What did Morgan say about it? "My celebration was more, 'That's the tea,' which is telling a story, spreading news." And more news followed: The U.S. claimed their fourth title, defeating the Netherlands, 2–0, in the final.

3. **Megan Rapinoe** had a memorable celebration in the 2019 quarterfinals after hitting the target against France (twice). The American struck a triumphant pose, chin up, arms outstretched. Later, she was named *Sports Illustrated* 2019 Sportsperson of the Year.

"It just feels right for the moment," said Rapinoe after the game. "I'm generally pretty off-the-cuff so I change [celebrations] up a lot, but this just felt right in this moment."

4

5. This way to celebrate a goal never happened at the 2023 Women's World Cup, but it could have. More than once after scoring, **Sam Kerr** of Australia has performed a backward somersault in the air. It's a skill she taught herself when she was nine years old.

"I've always said, whenever I do a backflip, it's not planned," Kerr shared at a press conference ahead of the World Cup in 2023. "It's just a bit of fun. It's about entertainment and having fun and showing what football's about." After the 2023 tournament, however, Kerr hinted her joyful acrobatics might be a thing of the past. "I turned 30 a month ago," she noted.

5

4. In 2007, England—finally qualifying for the World Cup after 12 years—faced Japan in the group stage. With 10 minutes on the clock and Japan up 1–0, **Kelly Smith** spun and netted an equalizer with her left foot. She celebrated her first World Cup goal by removing and kissing her left boot. Just two minutes later, Smith scored with her right foot. This time, she took off and kissed both boots to mark the amazing feat. The game ended in a draw, but every goal deserves to be celebrated.

"I actually got into quite a bit of trouble after the game with my head coach," Smith confessed years after. "I was told never to do that celebration again, so that was a once off."

15 TOP WOMEN'S WORLD CUP "GOOOOOAL!" SCORERS

More than 1,000 goals have been scored at nine Women's World Cups. That total does not include penalty shootouts. These records are likely to stand for a while as these players are all retired.

Player	Nation	WC Matches	WC Goals
Marta	Brazil	23	17
Birgit Prinz	Germany	24	14
Abby Wambach	U.S.	25	
Michelle Akers	U.S.	13	12
Sun Wen	China	20	11
Cristiane	Brazil	21	
Bettina Wiegmann	Germany	22	
Ann Kristin Aarones	Norway	11	10
Heidi Mohr	Germany	12	
Christine Sinclair	Canada	24	
Carli Lloyd	U.S.	25	
Linda Medalen	Norway	17	9
Megan Rapinoe	U.S.	20	
Alex Morgan	U.S.	22	
Hege Riise	Norway	22	

4 FLUBS, MISSES, AND OWN GOALS

Mistakes happen, even at the highest level of competition, like the World Cup. Flubs, misses, and own goals can become defining moments for a team. Other times, they're just painful.

1. "A moment of horror for the goalkeeper. A moment of unlikely joy for the United States," the commentator declared during the 2010 World Cup in South Africa. With England up 1–0 in the 40th minute, goalkeeper **Robert Green** had made a costly mistake. He had failed to save a long-range shot from U.S. midfielder Clint Dempsey. The ball bounced off his gloves and rolled across the goal line and into the net. The opening match of the tournament ended in a 1–1 draw.

"I'm sure there's 50-odd million people disappointed with me this evening," Green said after the match. "But I'll come back tomorrow, work hard in training, work hard the next day, prepare the same, prepare as if I'm playing in the next game and it won't affect me." Green didn't play for England again until the following year, when he kept a clean sheet in a friendly against Norway.

2. In her World Cup debut, **Laia Codina** of Spain scored twice against Switzerland in 2023. Her first goal, however, was more nightmarish than dreamy. In the 11th minute, Codina overpowered a back pass from the midfield to the keeper, who was out of position. Goalkeeper Cata Coll, also in her first-ever national team appearance, raced back to recover. But the ball bounced into the Spain goal, leveling the score at 1–1. Both players were despondent, but Codina's second goal, just before halftime, was a dream come true, finding the back of the correct net. Spain cruised to a 5–1 victory, advancing to the quarterfinals and ultimately winning the tournament.

4. At the 2010 World Cup, the match ball itself—the Jabulani—seemed to have caused some flubs and a few misses. Its design featured eight molded panels and a patterned surface for smoother flight. Goalkeepers hated the Jabulani. Spain's Iker Casillas compared it to a beach ball. Gianluigi Buffon called the ball "absolutely inadequate." Hugo Lloris of France described the design "a disaster." Uruguay striker **Diego Forlán**, however, thrived on the newly designed ball, scoring five goals in seven matches and winning the Golden Ball. What was the secret? Three months before the tournament, Forlán had requested a Jabulani ball from the manufacturer to practice with.

3. In the 2006 World Cup, the Italian goalkeeper **Gianluigi Buffon** conceded only one goal from open play. But it was an unusual one. The goal was scored by his own teammate, **Cristian Zaccardo**. The Italian defender badly mishit a U.S. free kick with his left ankle—into his team's net. The chaotic match ended in a 1–1 draw.

"Now that so much time has passed, I can joke about it," Zaccardo reflected on the slip-up a decade later. "The unexpected is always around the corner in football, like missing a penalty or scoring an own goal you'd never done until that day." Despite the own goal, Italy went on to win the tournament, and Buffon earned the Golden Glove.

ARE YOU ON THE BALL?
12 OFFICIAL WORLD CUP DESIGNS

Most World Cups have had official match balls. The design and look of the balls has advanced through the years. Here's the rollout.

1. ITALY 1934
FEDERALE 102

The Federale 102 had cotton instead of leather laces to make heading the ball more comfortable.

2. FRANCE 1938
ALLEN

The French company that made the Allen ball was one of the first to market its product.

3. BRAZIL 1950
SUPERBALL DUPLO T

The Superball Duplo T was the first soccer ball without any laces at all.

4. CHILE 1962
CRACK

The unusual-looking Crack ball was stitched with 18 irregular panels.

5. WEST GERMANY 1974
TELSTAR DURLAST

The Telstar Durlast followed the original Telstar, the first official World Cup ball in 1970. This version featured improved technology that made the ball more resistant to water.

6. MEXICO 1986
AZTECA

The Azteca, the first World Cup ball decorated (and named) in honor of the host nation, featured ancient Aztec designs.

7. FRANCE (MEN'S) 1998
UNITED STATES (WOMEN'S) 1999
TRICOLORE

The Tricolore, named after the blue, white, and red on French flag, was the first colored World Cup ball. A different design of the Tricolore, called the Icon, was the first match ball created for a Women's World Cup. The 1999 ball featured artwork of U.S. landmarks, including the Statue of Liberty.

8. JAPAN AND SOUTH KOREA (MEN'S) 2002
UNITED STATES (WOMEN'S) 2003
FEVERNOVA

The Fevernova, the last handsewn World Cup ball, is named for Asia's passion for the game. A version of the Fevernova appeared at the Women's World Cup in 2003.

9. SOUTH AFRICA (MEN'S) 2010
GERMANY (WOMEN'S) 2011
JABULANI

The Jabulani's 11 colors represent the 11 players on a soccer team and South Africa's 11 languages. Some players complained that the heat-sealed ball was too light and curvy. A different design of the Jabulani, called the Speed Cell, was the official match ball of the 2011 Women's World Cup.

10. BRAZIL 2014
BRAZUCA

The Brazuca was the first World Cup match ball named by the fans. *Brazuca* is a word that describes national pride in the Brazilian way of life.

11. QATAR 2022
AL RIHLA

The Al Rihla, made with water-based inks and glues, is the first environmentally friendly World Cup soccer ball.

12. AUSTRALIA AND NEW ZEALAND (WOMEN'S) 2023
OCEAUNZ FINAL PRO

The Oceaunz Final Pro, the color of sunsets in Sydney, Australia, appeared in the final four Women's World Cup matches in 2023.

36 COLD, HARD FACTS ABOUT INJURIES ON (AND OFF) THE PITCH

1. The most common injury on a soccer field is ankle sprain.

2. Minor strains may heal in a few days.

3. Serious injuries like torn ligaments or fractures can sideline a soccer player for months.

4. Playing soccer involves sudden changes in direction that can stress the knee, sometimes damaging the ACL.

5. The ACL, the anterior cruciate ligament, runs diagonally through the center of the knee.

6. Many soccer players, including Rodri from Spain and Catarina Macario from the U.S., have torn their ACLs, with recovery taking up to a year.

7. A recent study about soccer players found women are two to six times more likely to suffer ACL injuries than men.

8. There is less research on sports-related injuries in women compared to men.

9. One study suggested a possible reason for ACL injuries in women footballers could be the lack of footwear designed specifically for them.

10. Head injuries account for between 4 and 22 percent of all soccer injuries.

11. Many American players, such as Briana Scurry and Taylor Twellman, experienced concussions that disrupted their careers.

12. Signs of a concussion include confusion, dizziness, and headache.

13. Concussions are caused by knocks, bumps, or blows to the head (or body, neck, or shoulders).

14. Pro soccer players who have a concussion can't return to the field until they are free of symptoms and cleared by a doctor.

15. The more competitive the level of play, the more likely concussions are to occur.

16. Soccer players are more likely to get a concussion from colliding with other players than from heading the ball.

17. But heading a soccer ball is always risky.

18. In 2015, the U.S. Soccer Federation began limiting heading for players age 13 and younger.

19. Today, U.S. Soccer bans heading for players age 10 and younger. For players between ages 11 and 13, the organization permits heading only during games.

20. One report found slightly deflated soccer balls could reduce risk of head injuries by as much as 20 percent.

21. It's safer to head balls that are dry than balls that are wet because they are lighter.

22. Subbing in dry balls when it's wet out isn't a bad idea.

23. Playing a 90-minute soccer match puts a lot of strain on the body's ability to control its temperature.

24. Heat illness occurs when the body overheats, leading to symptoms like headaches, fatigue, and cramps.

25. Heat stress is most dangerous for high-level athletes; it's difficult to cool down during competitive tournaments that span several days.

26. Drinking fluids, ice towels, shade, and rest helps footballers recover from heat illness.

27. Water is the best drink to rehydrate.

28. Playing on artificial grass, or turf, puts extra stress on the joints. So it takes longer to recover from games on turf than on natural grass.

29. Turf exposes soccer players to more toxins and increases the risk of heat stress.

30. Playing on turf can also cause painful turf burns.

31. Video gaming can cause injuries that sideline players in real life. A pro footballer once had to miss a game due to knee pain after playing on the PlayStation with his foot on the coffee table for too long.

32. Another time, an English goalkeeper dropped a bottle of salad dressing on his toe. He was out for two months.

33. A Swedish footballer broke his jaw after biting on a carrot—but don't stop eating vegetables. He had gotten a knock on the jaw previously during a game.

34. Professional athletes have to be cautious, even on break. A backup goalkeeper from Scotland was once struck by a cow at his father's farm. He was out a couple of weeks with a shoulder injury.

35. No matter what the cause of injury, ice baths reduce muscle damage and pain in elite players, which may help in recovery.

36. It's not recommended that athletes stay in an ice bath longer than 15 or 20 minutes.

24 FOOTBALLER QUOTES YOU NEED TO HEAR

1. "You owe it to yourself to be the best you can be." **Christian Pulisic**

2. "My coach said I ran like a girl. I said if he could run a little faster, he could too." **Mia Hamm**

3. "I grew up playing basketball. I didn't really focus on soccer until I realized, yeah, I'm probably going to be too small to play basketball. But a lot of my instincts, how I'm always on my toes, how I defend, are almost like basketball. Being able to shuffle, being able to close down spaces. I'm always anticipating things." **Tyler Adams**

4. "It's hard to beat someone who never gives up." **Megan Rapinoe**

5. "Sometimes in football, you have to score goals." **Thierry Henry**

6. "I just want to be Jude and go on my own path." **Jude Bellingham**

7. "I just revel in those moments: having that huge crowd with all those crazy fans and millions watching on TV, being in the spotlight when so often women in sports are not. That's an incredible stage to be on." **Megan Rapinoe**

8. "It's not about how big you are. It's about how big you play." **Mallory Swanson**

9. "Only those who have the courage to take a penalty miss them." **Roberto Baggio**

10. "Honestly, I've just been trying to improve all parts of my game. A statistic is just a statistic." **Lindsey (Horan) Heaps**

11. "Maybe an orange card could be shown that sees a player go out of the game for 10 minutes for incidents that are not heavy enough for a red card." **Marco van Basten**

12. "The goalkeeper always starts again at nil, even when you're 2–0 down. It always starts again at scratch. It's a completely mental thing, and I keep reminding myself of it during matches." **Manuel Neuer**

13. "I was fast, but I wasn't the fastest. I was good in the air, but I wasn't the best. I could strike with both feet, but I wasn't the best. I had quality, but I wasn't the best. One thing that greatly helped me, though, was the fact that I had played basketball in my youth. … There's nothing better than basketball to lose your marker." **Just Fontaine**

14. "It's so valuable to learn that when you put yourself in an uncomfortable situation, you'll be fine, and you'll probably come out even stronger." **Julie Foudy**

15. "It's so meaningful and inspiring to see someone where you want to be. It's hard to imagine it, set that goal down, and really work towards it until you see it." **Naomi Girma**

16. "We have to stand up for what we believe in." **Weston McKennie**

17. "The ball has always been a life companion, my best friend." **Ronaldinho**

18. "I never want to be perceived as ungrateful or stuck-up, that's not who I am." **Trinity Rodman**

19. "I never scored a goal in my life without getting a pass from someone else." **Abby Wambach**

20. "Football is simple, but the hardest thing is to play simple football." **Johan Cruyff**

21. "My father is strong in his legs, and I think I get that from him. I am stronger there than in my upper body, but that is what gives me a low center of gravity. It makes it harder for opponents to get me off the ball." **Luka Modric**

22. "Everyone who knows me knows that I always eat cake. My nutritionist hates it, but I just tell her I like to eat it, and she's not going to stop me." **Lucy Bronze**

23. "I like lots of Korean music that most people have probably never heard of. I also enjoy hip-hop." **Son Heung-min**

24. "Sleep is very important." **Erling Haaland**

HOW TO BE A WORLD CUP FANATIC

42 WILD FAN FACTS

1. Soccer fans often paint their faces and bodies in their national flag colors to support their country's team.

2. Fans in the Netherlands are known for wearing orange, the traditional color of the Dutch royal family.

3. An orange suit is one thing. What about a hat topped with carrots too?

4. Passionate Danes turned out in red-and-white baseball caps at the 1986 World Cup in Mexico.

5. The Danish hat has flaps and strings to make it clap. It's called a *klaphat*.

6. For those who don't like headwear, a "soccer head" haircut makes a big statement.

7. Rattles used to be a popular way to cheer on your team from the stands.

8. In the early 20th century, fans brought rosettes—decorations made of ribbons—to soccer matches to support their side.

9. Soccer scarves first appeared at English matches in the 1930s.

10. Scarves have been an essential accessory since the 1970s. They keep a football fan warm and express team pride.

11. A long scarf in your country or club colors helps your team see support in the stadium.

12. Drums, chants, flags, and signs with funny messages for favorite players are other ways to show support.

13. The English club Manchester United once claimed to have over 650 million fans around the world. That's almost twice as many people as live in the entire U.S.

14. These days, everyone agrees the club with the most supporters is Spanish giant Real Madrid.

15. Blowing plastic horns called vuvuzelas, a part of African football culture, inspires players on the field.

16. Before South Africa hosted the World Cup in 2010, some coaches and players called for a ban on the loud vuvuzelas. They argued the constant noise was a distraction.

17. Although FIFA allowed vuvuzelas at the 2010 World Cup, it later banned the noisemakers from large tournaments.

18. Soccer fans can be fervent.

19. Colombians once showed their love for their men's coach, José Pékerman, by casting over 400,000 write-in votes for him as president.

20. It happened the day after Colombia defeated Greece in 2014 World Cup group play—the country's first win in a World Cup game in 16 years.

21. A *tifo* is a colorful visual display from fans at the start of a match, often involving flags, banners, or signs.

22. After winning it first World Cup in 2011—defeating the U.S. in the final—the Japanese women's national team held up a different kind of tifo.

23. The Japanese team expressed appreciation for fan support following a deadly earthquake and tsunami in their country.

24. Japanese goalkeeper Ayumi Kaihori later said: "We played that tournament not only for ourselves. We felt we had not only the support of Japan, but also the whole world."

25. *Tifo* comes from the Italian word for typhus, or fever, symbolizing intense, passionate support.

26. During the 2002 World Cup, dedicated Koreans displayed a tifo of their national flag, called the Taegeukgi.

27. The massive Korean flag cost more than $12,000 to make.

28. Moving this tifo required more than 40 people.

29. During the 2020 pandemic, many matches were played without spectators.

30. For one German team, more than 10,000 supporters paid to have cardboard cutouts of themselves placed in the stadium seats in 2021.

31. A spokesperson explained: "It's a good feeling for the players. It's a statement for us: the fans are part of the game."

32. Football fandom may sometimes be rewarded.

33. After Chelsea won the 2006 Premier League title, manager José Mourinho tossed two medals into the jubilant crowd.

34. The two fans who caught the medals later sold them for $25,000 and $40,000. Lucky ducks.

35. Supporters of one football team in Paris, France, got free tickets for a month—at a loss to the club of $1 million.

36. The club said the effort paid off through increased T-shirt sales and sponsorships.

37. In 2015, the U.S. women's national team received a New York City ticker-tape parade after winning its third World Cup.

38. Another New York City ticker-tape parade took place in 2019.

39. A crowd of 300,000 supporters turned out on a Wednesday morning to cheer for the team and its fourth Women's World Cup title.

40. People rock wild wigs, oversized glasses, and even animal costumes at soccer matches.

41. Everyone shows team spirit in their own way.

42. Some football fans attended a World Cup dressed as Smurfs. Just for the fun of it!

12 EXCELLENT QUESTIONS ABOUT SOCCER TRADITIONS

1. Why do players walk out with children before each World Cup match?

The tradition of so-called player escorts began at the 2002 World Cup, as part of the United Nations Children's Fund (UNICEF) "Say Yes for Children" initiative. The young escorts help remind soccer fans that "they have a major role to play in building a world fit for children," says the program.

2. What's the stuff that looks like shaving cream referees use on the grass?

It's called vanishing foam or spray. Referees use it for free kicks. Players must stand at least 10 yards (9 meters) away from the ball until it is kicked. The line on the grass marks that distance for the players. A foam line appeared for the first time at the 2014 World Cup—and disappeared about a minute later, after the kick.

3. Why do soccer teams change sides at halftime?

Soccer teams change sides at halftime to make sure things like wind, sun, and field conditions don't favor one side. If the game goes into extra time, they switch again between the two 15-minute halves.

4. Why do players celebrate a goal by pretending to shine shoes?

You have to clean the boot to take another shot and score again. It's a bit of a superstition and also a way to show respect for the goal scorer.

5. What's wrong with time wasting?

Time wasting is when players slow down the game on purpose. They might take too long on kicks or stay down after a minor injury to run down the clock. A player or a team might waste time when they are trying to protect a lead. Many say they prefer to watch goals being scored. Others say it's just part of the game.

6. Why do some footballers have holes in their socks?

Soccer players sometimes cut holes in their socks to reduce pressure on their calf muscles. Jude Bellingham of England was one of the first players to turn his kit to Swiss cheese. Whatever works!

7. Why do footballers take a drink of water and then spit it out instead of swallowing it?

Those players may be carb rinsing. This practice involves swishing a sugary and salty sports drink in the mouth to trick the brain into thinking extra energy is coming. This delays fatigue signals, giving athletes a short boost in performance. Or those spitters might just be trying to gross us out.

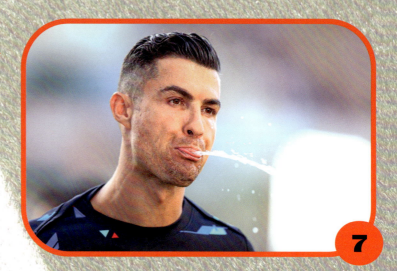

8. Why do they call corner kicks "set pieces"?

Set pieces are set plays, which teams can plan and practice in advance. A set piece happens when the ball is put back in play after a stoppage. Examples include corner kicks, penalty kicks, goal kicks, and throw-ins. A well-executed set piece can lead to a goal and often makes the difference between winning or losing. Recent trends show that up to 30 percent of goals come from or right after set pieces.

9. Why do footballers raise their arms before taking a corner kick?

When the player about to take a corner kick raises one (or two) arms, they are signaling to their teammates where they plan to kick the ball. It's part of a well-executed set piece.

10. Why does one soccer player often lie down on free kicks?

You might have noticed one player lying down behind the defensive wall just before the opponent takes a free kick. The tactic is simple: it prevents the kicker from shooting the ball underneath the wall while the players jump. The player on the ground is a block against low shots.

11. Why do players swap shirts at the end of a game?

Players sometimes trade their jerseys at the end of a match as a sign of respect. It's a tradition, especially between players who admire each other's skills.

12. What is the difference between the Best FIFA Player of the Year and the Ballon d'Or awards?

Both awards honor the best men's and women's players each year. *France Football* magazine has organized the Ballon d'Or ("Golden Ball" in French) since 1956 for men and 2018 for women. Guess who awards the Best FIFA Player of the Year? FIFA reintroduced this award in 2016 after merging with the Ballon d'Or from 2010 to 2015. Many top players, including Lionel Messi, Cristiano Ronaldo, Megan Rapinoe, and Aitana Bonmatí, have won both awards.

24 OFFICIAL WORLD CUP MASCOTS

Mascots are the fun, colorful characters who engage with fans and support the teams. The first official World Cup mascot was introduced in 1966.

1. ENGLAND 1966
WORLD CUP WILLIE

Inspired by his son, a British illustrator sketched the first World Cup mascot in under five minutes. English fans embraced the lion in a Union Jack shirt. World Cup Willie appeared on T-shirts and tea towels.

2. MEXICO 1970
JUANITO

Juanito ("Little Juan") wore a straw hat called a sombrero and a green Mexico team jersey. A colorful mascot made perfect sense—1970 was the first year the World Cup matches were broadcast on TV in color.

3. WEST GERMANY 1974
TIP AND TAP

Football-loving Tip and Tap wore the host country's white shirts. One wore the letters *WM*, short for *Weltmeisterschaft* (German for "World Cup"). The other wore the year of the tournament—74.

4. ARGENTINA 1978
GAUCHITO

A cheerful young football fan in Argentina's kit was the fourth World Cup mascot. Gauchito resembled a South American gaucho, with a handkerchief and a cowboy-style hat.

5. SPAIN 1982
NARANJITO

For the 1982 World Cup, the mascot wasn't a person at all. It was a piece of talking fruit representing Spain—a smiling orange, clutching a football.

6. MEXICO 1986
PIQUE

Mexico's second mascot was a large chili pepper with arms, legs, and a moustache. Pique wore an oversized sombrero and an outfit matching Mexico's kit. (*Picante* means "spicy" in Spanish.)

7. ITALY 1990
CIAO

Ciao—named for the Italian greeting—was a modern stick figure with a football for a head. Its colors were the green, white, and red of Italy's flag. The faceless mascot failed to energize some football fans.

8. CHINA (WOMEN'S) 1991
LING LING

The mascot for the first Women's World Cup was a mythical bird called a phoenix. Ling Ling represented harmony, beauty, and longevity—a new beginning for international women's soccer.

9. UNITED STATES 1994
STRIKER

In 1994, the U.S. public voted for its World Cup mascot. Their selection? Striker, a scrappy dog with floppy ears, dressed in red, white, and blue, with cleats on his paws.

10. SWEDEN (WOMEN'S) 1995
FIFFI

The second Women's World Cup mascot was a Viking character named Fiffi. She sported the colors of the Swedish flag and a horned helmet, representing the seafaring Vikings of Scandinavia.

11. FRANCE 1998
FOOTIX

The Gallic rooster, or *le coq gaulois*, is a national symbol of France. The 1998 World Cup mascot was Footix—a traditional Gallic rooster with a blue body, red head, and yellow beak—holding a soccer ball, naturally.

12. UNITED STATES (WOMEN'S) 1999
NUTMEG

The third Women's World Cup mascot was a female fox, aptly named Nutmeg. This fox had speed and agility—the nutmegging skills needed to get past an opponent by passing the ball through their legs.

13. JAPAN AND SOUTH KOREA 2002
KAZ, ATO, AND NIK

These three shiny, horned creatures from outer space played a football-like sport called Atmoball. Kaz, Ato, and Nik were the first World Cup mascots of the 21st century. Their names were chosen at fast-food restaurants and online in the host nations.

14. UNITED STATES (WOMEN'S) 2003 (NONE, THOUGH HUA MULAN WAS THE ORIGINAL CHOICE)

There was no official mascot for this tournament after it was moved from China due to the outbreak of the SARS illness.

15. GERMANY 2006
GOLEO VI AND PILLE

Goleo VI was a furry lion in a shirt the colors of the host kit. Pille was a talking soccer ball. OK, fine, but fans wondered: Where are Goleo's trousers?

16. CHINA (WOMEN'S) 2007
HUA MULAN

China's second Women's World Cup featured a girl as its mascot. Inspired by an ancient Chinese heroine, this Hua Mulan wore cleats and carried a soccer ball. The story of Mulan has been adapted into films over the years.

17. SOUTH AFRICA 2010
ZAKUMI

Combine Z.A. (*Zuid-Afrika*, "South Africa" in Dutch) and *kumi* ("ten" in African languages) and you get Zakumi—a cheerful leopard with green hair—for the continent's first World Cup.

18. GERMANY (WOMEN'S) 2011
KARLA KICK

Karla Kick was a curious, sport-loving cat who carried a soccer ball with her. She didn't speak but connected with fans and players, regardless of culture or language, according to FIFA.

19. BRAZIL 2014
FULECO

Fuleco, a three-banded armadillo, combined the Portuguese *futebol* (football) and *ecologia* (ecology). The choice was meant to promote conservation, but some criticized the campaign for falling short.

20. CANADA (WOMEN'S) 2015
SHUÉME

Canada's mascot was a great white owl named Shuéme. Her name, inspired by the French word for owl (*chouette*), honored one of Canada's two official languages.

21. RUSSIA 2018
ZABIVAKA

Zabivaka means "the one who scores" in Russian. More than one million Russians chose this likeable wolf in an online poll as their World Cup mascot.

22. FRANCE (WOMEN'S) 2019
ETTIE

The bright yellow Ettie chicken was the daughter of the rooster Footix, the 1998 World Cup mascot. Her name comes from the French word for star—*étoile*.

23. QATAR 2022
LA'EEB

La'eeb means a "super-skilled player" in Arabic. The mascot was based on a traditional Qatari headdress called a ghutra.

24. AUSTRALIA AND NEW ZEALAND (WOMEN'S) 2023
TAZUNI

This soccer-loving mascot was based on the *Eudyptula minor*, the smallest penguin species that lives only in New Zealand and Australia. *Tazuni* was a fusion of the penguin's home, the Tasman Sea, and the word *unity*.

25 THINGS TO KNOW ABOUT SOCCER SWAG

1. A secret bidder forked over $225,000 in 2002 for Pelé's jersey from the 1970 World Cup final. It was the most expensive soccer jersey ever sold at the time.

2. A die-hard fan bought Geoff Hurst's red team jersey for $135,000 in 2000. (Hurst wore it netting the hat trick that clinched England's first and only World Cup win in 1966.)

3. In 2008, another buyer called Hurst's jersey "the most important shirt in English football history" and insured it for $2 million.

4. In 2016, Hurst's jersey, apparently overvalued, went unsold at an auction.

5. Mario Götze scored the winning goal for Germany in the 2014 World Cup final against Argentina. Four years later, one of his game boots sold for $2 million.

6. Remember Maradona's "hand of God" ball that sold at auction for nearly $2.4 million? The jersey he was wearing during

that game went for almost $9.3 million in 2022.

7. A drawing of the 1966 World Cup Willie mascot, signed by the artist, sold for only $400 in 2017. Only five years later, it had tripled in value.

8. Even a small stuffed version of the World Cup Willie lion requires more than $250.

9. Many World Cup items are affordable.

10. Before each tournament, special World Cup merchandise, including limited-edition bobbleheads and special silver coins, hits the (online) shelves.

11. Ahead of the 2023 Women's World Cup, supporters could buy small action figures of Rose Lavelle, bucket hats, and player bag clips.

12. U.S. soccer fans can purchase all kinds of branded gear, such as pet leashes and T-shirts with their own names on the back.

13. Some World Cup items are edible: U.S. Soccer Golden Goals, a Quaker Oats breakfast cereal, honored the 1999 women's champions.

14. Fans of football, like baseball, can collect trading cards of their favorite players.

15. Rookie cards sometimes end up being worth a lot.

16. A limited-edition cartoon-inspired card of Spanish star Lamine Yamal already sells for tens of thousands of dollars.

17. What about virtual trading cards? Many pro soccer clubs offer fans unique digital collectibles.

18. Digital cards capture cool player images or clips of impressive game-winning moments.

19. Lionel Messi, Luis Suárez, and Luciano Acosta had the top-three selling MLS jerseys for 2024.

20. The top-selling American jersey belonged to striker Jordan Morris, who ranked seventh for most MLS jerseys sold for 2024.

21. Alex Morgan had the best-selling NWSL jersey the year she retired (2024).

22. The Trinity Rodman and Sophia Smith (now Wilson) jerseys ranked second and third in sales.

23. Released in 2020, an Alex Morgan Barbie doll was fully posable, with removable cleats and its own soccer ball.

24. Looking for something more exciting than cards and bobbleheads? In 2022, around 140 Americans pooled their money to buy a third-tier soccer club outside of Copenhagen, Denmark.

25. Results for the struggling Danish club have been mixed, but the watch parties are fun. Every club needs supporters.

28 THINGS TO KNOW ABOUT CROWDS AND CUPS

1. Nothing compares to attending a World Cup match in person.

2. But watching it with fellow soccer fans (and pets) at home can be almost as thrilling.

3. By the way, pets are not permitted inside World Cup stadiums.

4. Musical instruments are also banned, as are hammers, drones, confetti, and umbrellas.

5. More than 765,000 fans visited Qatar in the first two weeks of the World Cup it hosted.

6. More than 3.4 million tickets overall were sold at the 2022 World Cup in Qatar—and that's not even a record-breaking total.

7. The 1994 World Cup in the United States holds the record for the highest overall attendance—3.6 million.

8. Nearly 2 million spectators in total attended the 2023 Women's World Cup.

9. In 2024, FIFA announced Brazil would be the first South American nation to host the Women's World Cup, in 2027.

10. The 2026 World Cup marked the first time in history that three nations were selected to host the tournament together.

11. The 2026 World Cup host nations—Canada, Mexico, and the United States—were named in 2018.

12. Sixteen stadiums were selected for the 2026 World Cup matches in 11 U.S. cities, three cities in Mexico, and two cities in Canada.

13. For Mexico, the selected 2026 World Cup cities were Guadalajara, Mexico City, and Monterrey.

14. For Canada, the selected 2026 World Cup cities were Toronto and Vancouver.

15. For the U.S., FIFA picked stadiums in Atlanta, Boston, Dallas, Houston, Kansas City, Los Angeles, Miami, New York/New Jersey, Philadelphia, the San Francisco Bay Area, and Seattle to host 2026 World Cup matches.

16. A stadium in East Rutherford, New Jersey, was awarded the 2026 World Cup final.

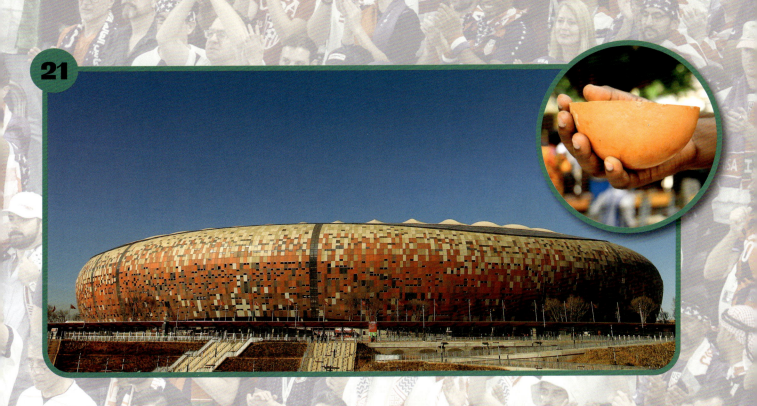

17. The "New York New Jersey Stadium" seats a total of 87,000 fans.

18. Due to FIFA's ban on corporate-sponsored names, many venues are temporarily renamed during the tournament.

19. No new stadiums were built just for the 2026 World Cup tournament.

20. Whatever stadium you might be in, watch out for the sun and the heat.

21. Soccer City in Johannesburg, South Africa, was inspired by the African water-carrying gourd known as a calabash. The stadium hosted the 2010 World Cup final.

22. The largest Women's World Cup final took place in 1999 at the Rose Bowl in Pasadena, California, with 90,185 spectators.

23. An astounding 173,850 spectators turned up to the 1950 World Cup final at Maracanã Stadium.

24. Some have said, from the sky, the circular stadium in Rio de Janeiro, Brazil, looks like a belly button.

25. The 1950 World Cup final still holds the record for largest crowd in World Cup history. (Uruguay beat host Brazil 2–1.)

26. Today, there is room for just under 79,000 fans in Maracanã Stadium after renovations reduced its capacity.

27. The 2014 World Cup final was also held in Maracanã Stadium in Rio de Janeiro, Brazil.

28. In 2024, Maracanã Stadium was also chosen to host the 2027 Women's World Cup final.

THE ROAD TO THE WORLD CUP

25 FACTS ABOUT FOOTBALL CONFEDERATIONS

1. FIFA has six football confederations worldwide.

2. Each confederation manages the game of soccer on its continent.

3. There's a confederation for Asia, Africa, Europe, South America, Oceania, and North America.

4. What about the seventh continent?

5. Antarctica, with no permanent population and no single governing nation, has no national team or FIFA confederation.

6. British icon David Beckham played football on Antarctica once. For a TV show, he captained a team of explorers on a glacier, with skis as goalposts.

7. The world's six football confederations organize their own national and club competitions.

8. The six football confederations also help their nations qualify for global tournaments—like the World Cup.

9. The football confederations are made up of member associations, or national football associations, responsible for soccer within their countries.

10. Concacaf manages the game of soccer in the United States, Canada, and Mexico, as well as Central America and the Caribbean.

11. If you try saying "Confederation of North, Central America and Caribbean Association Football" three times fast, you'll see why people call it Concacaf.

12. If you want to say it aloud, it's CON-kah-caff.

13. By the way, CONCACAF officially became "Concacaf" for marketing reasons in 2018.

14. The oldest Concacaf member is the Guyana Football Federation, founded in 1902.

15. Some confederations award Best Player titles each year.

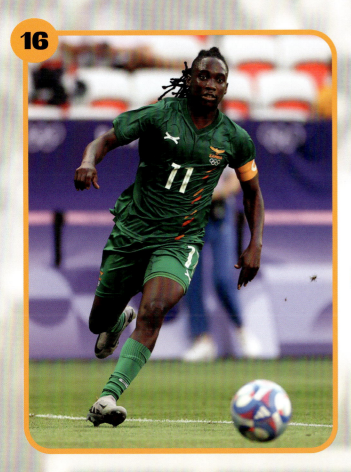

18. The AFC has fielded one World Cup winner: the women's team from Japan in 2011.

19. South America's CONMEBOL was the first confederation to begin its qualification for the 2026 World Cup—in 2023.

20. The first goal of the 2026 FIFA World Cup qualification was scored by Rafael Santos Borré (19) of Colombia, in a victory over Venezuela.

16. The Confederation of African Football (CAF) named Barbra Banda the Women's African Footballer of the Year in 2024. She was the first Zambian to win.

17. The Asian Football Confederation (AFC) has named Son Heung-min of South Korea the Asian International Player of the Year four times. That's more than any other footballer.

21. The Oceania Football Confederation (OFC) was guaranteed a qualification spot for the first time in 2026.

22. Of the six confederations, the European one gets the most direct slots for the women's and men's World Cup tournaments.

23. The professional leagues in Europe offer the highest level of competition.

24. Everyone wants the best teams from around the globe to battle it out for the World Cup.

25. Which continents have produced the most men's and women's World Cup champions? Europe and South America.

WHAT ARE THE 6 FOOTBALL CONFEDERATIONS? AND 6 EXTRA FOOTIE FACTS

Kick off with these footie facts about the FIFA confederations and associations.

1. AFC (Asian Football Confederation)

Year founded: 1954
Established in: Manila, Philippines
Member associations: 47
Notable competitions: AFC Asian Cup (women's and men's)
Players of the year (2023): Akram Afif (Qatar), Kiko Seike (Japan)

Extra footie fact: Though the nation is part of Oceania, Australia joined the Asian Football Confederation in 2006.

2. CAF (Confederation of African Football)

Year founded: 1957
Established in: Khartoum, Sudan
Member associations: 54
Notable competitions: Africa Cup of Nations (women's and men's)
Players of the year (2024): Barbra Banda (Zambia), Ademola Lookman (Nigeria)

Extra footie fact: Nigeria has the most women's Africa Cup of Nations titles, and Egypt tops the men's tournament.

4. CONMEBOL (South American Football Confederation)

Year founded: 1916
Established in: Buenos Aires, Argentina
Member associations: 10
Notable competitions: Copa América (women's and men's)
Players of the year (2024): Gabi Zanotti (Brazil), Luiz Henrique (Brazil)

Extra footie fact: CONMEBOL is a shortened version of the confederation's full name in Spanish: *Confederación Sudamericana de Fútbol*.

5. OFC (Oceania Football Confederation)

Year founded: 1966
Established in: Auckland, New Zealand
Member associations: 11, plus 2 associate members
Notable competitions: OFC Champions League (women's and men's), OFC Nations Cup (women's and men's)
Players of the year: None selected since 2015
Extra footie fact: FIFA doesn't recognize the small island nations of Kiribati and Tuvalu so they cannot qualify for the World Cup. They are only associate members of the OFC.

3. CONCACAF (Confederation of North, Central America and Caribbean Association Football)

Year founded: 1961
Established in: Mexico City, Mexico
Member associations: 41
Notable competitions: Concacaf Gold Cup (men's), Concacaf Nations League (men's), Concacaf W Gold Cup (women's), Concacaf W Championship (women's)
Players of the year (2023–24): Adalberto Carrasquilla (Panama), Melchie Dumornay (Haiti)

Extra footie fact: The U.S. Soccer Federation (U.S. Soccer), the Canadian Soccer Association (Canada Soccer), and the Mexican Football Federation (FMF) are members of Concacaf.

6. UEFA (Union of European Football Associations)

Year founded: 1954
Established in: Basel, Switzerland
Members: 55
Notable competitions: UEFA Euro (women's and men's), UEFA Nations League (women's and men's)
Players of the year: UEFA ended its own annual Best Player awards after teaming up with *France Football* for the Ballon d'Or.
Extra footie fact: Germany holds the most UEFA Women's Euro titles, and Spain tops the men's tournament.

TWO TABLES, ONE GOAL:
UNDERSTANDING WORLD CUP QUALIFYING

Not every nation makes it to the World Cup. Many are eliminated during qualification, which spans a few years. Each of the six confederations has its own way of awarding its direct slots. Each confederation's next-best team(s) then participate in a playoff for the remaining spots. The last spots are filled just months before the tournament starts. Host countries automatically qualify, with their spots coming from their confederation.

1. THE MEN'S WORLD CUP

Confederations	Direct Slots	Playoff Slots
AFC (Asia)	8	1
CAF (Africa)	9	1
Concacaf (North, Central America and the Caribbean)	6	2
CONMEBOL (South America)	6	1
OFC (Oceania)	1	1
UEFA (Europe)	16	0
Winners of playoff	2	–
TOTAL (2026)	48	

* = Hosts Canada, Mexico, and the United States qualified automatically, leaving three direct slots.

2. THE WOMEN'S WORLD CUP

Confederations	Direct Slots	Playoff Slots
AFC (Asia)	6	2
CAF (Africa)	4	2
Concacaf (North, Central America and the Caribbean)	4	2
CONMEBOL (South America)	3	2
OFC (Oceania)	1	1
UEFA (Europe)	11	1
Winners of playoff	3	–
TOTAL (2027)	32	

* = Host Brazil qualified automatically, leaving two direct slots.

21 FACTS ABOUT THE WORLD CUP DRAW

1. Each World Cup competition has a **group stage** and then a **knockout stage**.

2. After teams have qualified, FIFA places them in **pods**, based on their world ranking.

3. A random draw from each pod, held about six months before the tournament, determines the groups in the group stage.

4. The group with the strongest teams is often called the Group of Death. No dying is involved, of course.

5. Teams in each group play a **round robin**: each team plays each other team once.

6. Losses in the group stage do not immediately eliminate teams.

7. It's possible to play a team in both the group stage and the knockout stage.

8. In the group stage, teams **earn points**: three for a win, one for a tie, and zero for a loss.

9. The top teams from each group based on those points move on to the knockout stage.

10. Ties in a group are settled by **goal differential** (total team goals scored minus those given up).

11. To maintain fairness, the final two group stage matches are played at the same time.

12. FIFA created this rule after a last group stage match at the 1982 World Cup.

13. In a 1982 group stage match between West Germany and Austria, both teams knew that a 1–0 German win would be enough to advance (and eliminate Algeria).

14. After Horst Hrubesch of West Germany scored in the 10th minute, the two teams just passed around the ball for the rest of the match. Fans were not happy.

15. Matches in the knockout round require a winner. If needed, extra time or penalties decide who wins and who gets "knocked out."

16. There are at least four knockout rounds in a World Cup competition. (The 2026 World Cup bracket was set at five knockout rounds.)

17. There are 16 teams in the **Round of 16**. Winners advance to the quarterfinals.

18. There are eight teams in the **quarterfinals**, with the winners advancing to the semifinals.

19. There are four teams in the **semifinals**, with the winners advancing to the final.

20. The winning team in the **final** becomes the World Cup champions. But you knew that.

21. The losers of the semifinals face off against each other for **third place**.

WHICH 32 COUNTRIES BOOKED THEIR TICKETS TO THE MEN'S WORLD CUP?
AND 32 EXTRA FOOTIE FACTS

When a team "books their ticket" to the World Cup, it means they've earned the right to play in the tournament. These 32 countries competed in the 2022 World Cup in Qatar. The men's tournament expands to 48 teams in 2026. Tackle these footie facts about the countries.

ARGENTINA

Where in the world: South America
Capital city: Buenos Aires
Population: 46,994,384
What people speak: Spanish, Italian, English, German
FIFA confederation: CONMEBOL (South American Football Confederation)
Extra footie fact: Even after taking home the 2022 World Cup, Argentina was ranked second behind Brazil by FIFA. Why? The complex ranking formula includes winning individual matches, not tournaments. Teams get fewer points for winning on penalties rather than in normal or extra time.

AUSTRALIA

Where in the world: Island continent southeast of Asia, surrounded by Indian Ocean and Pacific Ocean
Capital city: Canberra
Population: 26,768,598
What people speak: English, Chinese (Mandarin, Cantonese), Arabic
FIFA confederation: AFC (Asian Football Confederation)
Extra footie fact: The men's Aussie team call themselves the Socceroos. It's a blend of the word *soccer* and a certain hopping animal native to the country.

BELGIUM

Where in the world: Western Europe
Capital city: Brussels
Population: 11,977,634
What people speak: Dutch, French, German
FIFA confederation: UEFA (Union of European Football Associations)
Extra footie fact: The Belgian national team has speakers of Dutch and French, among other languages. On the field, they often switch to English as a common language.

BRAZIL

Where in the world: South America
Capital city: Brasília
Population: 220,051,512
What people speak: Portuguese
FIFA confederation: CONMEBOL (South American Football Confederation)
Extra footie fact: Brazil is the only country to have participated in every World Cup.

CAMEROON

Where in the world: Central Africa
Capital city: Yaoundé
Population: 30,966,105
What people speak: English, French
FIFA confederation: CAF (Confederation of African Football)
Extra footie fact: In 1972, Cameroon's first president gave the national team a new name—the Indomitable Lions. For obvious reasons: *indomitable* means "impossible to defeat," and lion is Cameroon's national animal.

CANADA

Where in the world: North America
Capital city: Ottawa
Population: 38,794,813
What people speak: English, French, Chinese languages, Spanish
FIFA confederation: Concacaf (Confederation of North, Central America and Caribbean Association Football)
Extra footie fact: As a host nation, Canada was one of the first teams to book its ticket to the 2026 World Cup.

COSTA RICA

Where in the world: Central America
Capital city: San José
Population: 5,265,575
What people speak: Spanish, English
FIFA confederation: Concacaf (Confederation of North, Central America and Caribbean Association Football)
Extra footie fact: Costa Rica was the last country to qualify for the 2022 World Cup. It edged out New Zealand.

CROATIA

Where in the world: Southeastern Europe
Capital city: Zagreb
Population: 4,150,116
What people speak: Croatian
FIFA confederation: UEFA (Union of European Football Associations)
Extra footie fact: Since its first World Cup in 1998, Croatia has reached the podium twice. The country finished second in 2018 and third in 2022.

DENMARK

Where in the world: Northern Europe
Capital city: Copenhagen
Population: 5,973,136
What people speak: Danish, Faroese, Greenlandic (Inuit dialect), English
FIFA confederation: UEFA (Union of European Football Associations)
Extra footie fact: At its first World Cup in 1986, Denmark reached the Round of 16. In 1998, they made it to the quarterfinals, where they lost to Brazil. The Denmark national team also represents Greenland.

ECUADOR

Where in the world: South America
Capital city: Quito
Population: 18,309,984
What people speak: Spanish (Castilian), Indigenous (including Quechua)
FIFA confederation: CONMEBOL (South American Football Confederation)
Extra footie fact: Ecuador has never advanced to the knockout stage of the World Cup, but again, there is always the next time.

ENGLAND

Where in the world: Western Europe
Capital city: London
Population: 57,112,500
What people speak: English, Cornish
FIFA confederation: UEFA (Union of European Football Associations)
Extra footie fact: England, Wales, Scotland, and Northern Ireland make up the United Kingdom, but FIFA recognizes them as separate teams. Fans are so enthusiastic, merging the teams into one might break up the nation.

FRANCE

Where in the world: Western Europe
Capital city: Paris
Population: 68,374,591
What people speak: French, regional dialects and languages
FIFA confederation: UEFA (Union of European Football Associations)
Extra footie fact: For their exciting and positive style of play, the French team won the FIFA Most Entertaining Team Award, chosen by the public, in 1998.

GERMANY

Where in the world: Central Europe
Capital city: Berlin
Population: 84,119,100
What people speak: German, Danish, Frisian, Sorbian
FIFA confederation: UEFA (Union of European Football Associations)
Extra footie fact: Germany and Italy have each won the World Cup four times, but Germany has qualified more times than any other European nation.

GHANA

Where in the world: West Africa
Capital city: Accra
Population: 34,589,092
What people speak: Asante, Ewe, Fante, Boron (Brong)
FIFA confederation: CAF (Confederation of African Football)
Extra footie fact: Ghana might have been the first African team to reach the semifinals if Uruguay's Luis Suárez hadn't blocked a last-minute goal with his hand in 2010. Asamoah Gyan missed the resulting penalty, and Ghana went on to lose in a heartbreaking shootout.

IRAN

Where in the world: Middle East
Capital city: Tehran
Population: 88,386,937
What people speak: Persian Farsi (official), Azeri and other Turkic dialects, Kurdish
FIFA confederation: AFC (Asian Football Confederation)
Extra footie fact: In 2022, Iran competed in its third World Cup in a row. It lost to the United States in the group stage.

JAPAN

Where in the world: East Asia
Capital city: Tokyo
Population: 123,201,945
What people speak: Japanese
FIFA confederation: AFC (Asian Football Confederation)
Extra footie fact: In March 2025, Japan became the first nation to book their ticket to the 2026 World Cup through confederation qualifying.

MEXICO

Where in the world: North America
Capital city: Mexico City
Population: 130,739,927
What people speak: Spanish, Indigenous languages (including Mayan and Nahuatl)
FIFA confederation: Concacaf (Confederation of North, Central America and Caribbean Association Football)
Extra footie fact: Mexico City's Azteca Stadium is the location of the first game of the 2026 World Cup.

MOROCCO

Where in the world: North Africa
Capital city: Rabat
Population: 37,387,585
What people speak: Arabic, Tamazight languages, French
FIFA confederation: CAF (Confederation of African Football)
Extra footie fact: The first north African nation to host the World Cup will be Morocco. Look for them at the 2030 World Cup, along with cohosts Spain and Portugal (and Uruguay, Argentina, and Paraguay).

NETHERLANDS

Where in the world: Western Europe
Capital city: Amsterdam
Population: 17,772,378
What people speak: Dutch
FIFA confederation: UEFA (Union of European Football Associations)
Extra footie fact: The third time isn't always the charm. The Netherlands reached the World Cup finals in 1974, 1978, and 2010, but they've never lifted the trophy.

POLAND

Where in the world: Central Europe
Capital city: Warsaw
Population: 38,746,310
What people speak: Polish
FIFA confederation: UEFA (Union of European Football Associations)
Extra footie fact: Robert Lewandowski is the only Poland player to have won the Best FIFA Men's Player. Twice. He scored his 700th senior career goal (club and country) in 2024. But in World Cup play, he has netted only two goals.

PORTUGAL

Where in the world: Southern Europe
Capital city: Lisbon
Population: 10,207,177
What people speak: Portuguese, Mirandese
FIFA confederation: UEFA (Union of European Football Associations)
Extra footie fact: One of the greatest comebacks in World Cup history took place in 1966. Portugal came back from 3–0 down in the first 25 minutes to beat North Korea 5–3.

QATAR

Where in the world: Middle East
Capital city: Doha
Population: 2,552,088
What people speak: Arabic, English
FIFA confederation: AFC (Asian Football Confederation)
Extra footie fact: The day Qatar won its bid to host the 2022 World Cup, it also won a spot to participate. That was twelve years before the tournament began. World Cup host nations have qualified automatically since 1938.

SAUDI ARABIA

Where in the world: Middle East
Capital city: Riyadh
Population: 36,544,431
What people speak: Arabic
FIFA confederation: AFC (Asian Football Confederation)
Extra footie fact: In Saudi Arabia, for every five people under the age of 30, only one doesn't play, attend, or follow soccer. The country is set to host the 2034 World Cup.

SENEGAL

Where in the world: West Africa
Capital city: Dakar
Population: 18,847,519
What people speak: French, Wolof, Pular, Jola
FIFA confederation: CAF (Confederation of African Football)
Extra footie fact: After Cameroon in 1990, Senegal was the first African nation to reach a quarterfinal, in 2002. It was their first World Cup appearance.

SERBIA

Where in the world: Southeastern Europe
Capital city: Belgrade
Population: 6,652,212
What people speak: Serbian, Hungarian, Romani
FIFA confederation: UEFA (Union of European Football Associations)
Extra footie fact: The eagle has landed: the Serbian national team, known as the *Orlovi* (Eagles), takes their name from the majestic bird on their flag.

SOUTH KOREA

Where in the world: East Asia
Capital city: Seoul
Population: 52,081,799
What people speak: Korean, English
FIFA confederation: AFC (Asian Football Confederation)
Extra footie fact: At the 2022 World Cup, South Korea (world ranking: 40) knocked out football powerhouses Italy (6) and Spain (8) before losing to Germany, 1–0. It was the first time in World Cup history a nation outside Europe and the Americas reached the semifinals.

SPAIN

Where in the world: Southern Europe
Capital city: Madrid
Population: 47,280,433
What people speak: Castilian Spanish, Catalan, Galician, Basque
FIFA confederation: UEFA (Union of European Football Associations)
Extra footie fact: In 2010, Spain became the first nation to win the World Cup after losing the first match of the tournament. In the 2022 World Cup, Spain was upset by Morocco in a game that ended on penalties. Spain's loss made Morocco the first Arab nation to reach a World Cup quarterfinal.

SWITZERLAND

Where in the world: Western Europe
Capital city: Bern
Population: 8,860,574
What people speak: German, French, Italian, Romansh
FIFA confederation: UEFA (Union of European Football Associations)
Extra footie fact: The highest scoring match in World Cup history took place in 1954, when Switzerland defeated Austria, 7–5. It might have been an even higher scoreline, had Austria not missed a penalty in the first half.

TUNISIA

Where in the world: North Africa
Capital city: Tunis
Population: 12,048,847
What people speak: Arabic, French, Tamazight
FIFA confederation: CAF (Confederation of African Football)
Extra footie fact: Tunisia has never advanced to the knockout stage of the World Cup, but there is always the next time.

UNITED STATES

Where in the world: North America
Capital city: Washington, D.C.
Population: 341,963,408
FIFA confederation: Concacaf (Confederation of North, Central America and Caribbean Association Football)
What people speak: English, Spanish, Hawaiian, other Indigenous languages
Extra footie fact: U.S. ticket to the 2026 World Cup: already booked. Another good reason to host.

URUGUAY

Where in the world: South America
Capital city: Montevideo
Population: 3,425,330
What people speak: Spanish
FIFA confederation: CONMEBOL (South American Football Confederation)
Extra footie fact: Uruguay didn't just host the first-ever World Cup, in 1930, they won it too. But most impressive, they were the smallest nation to ever win (1930 Population: 1.5 million).

WALES

Where in the world: Western Europe
Capital city: Cardiff
Population: 3,132,700
What people speak: English, Welsh
FIFA confederation: UEFA (Union of European Football Associations)
Extra footie fact: After participating in its first World Cup in 1958, Wales took 64 years to reach its second Cup.

WHICH 32 COUNTRIES BOOKED THEIR TICKETS TO THE WOMEN'S WORLD CUP?
AND 32 EXTRA FOOTIE FACTS

These countries qualified for—or booked tickets to—the 2023 Women's World Cup in Australia and New Zealand. Here are some footie facts about them. The women's tournament could expand to 48 teams in 2031, when the U.S., with Concacaf partners, is set to host the Women's World Cup. Game on.

ARGENTINA

Where in the world: South America
Capital city: Buenos Aires
Population: 46,994,384
What people speak: Spanish, Italian, English, German
FIFA confederation: CONMEBOL (South American Football Confederation)
Extra footie fact: Argentina played in its first Women's World Cup in 2003.

BRAZIL

Where in the world: South America
Capital city: Brasília
Population: 220,051,512
What people speak: Portuguese
FIFA confederation: CONMEBOL (South American Football Confederation)
Extra footie fact: As the host nation, Brazil has already qualified to be one of the 24 teams at the 2027 Women's World Cup.

AUSTRALIA

Where in the world: Island continent southeast of Asia, surrounded by Indian Ocean and Pacific Ocean
Capital city: Canberra
Population: 26,768,598
What people speak: English, Chinese (Mandarin, Cantonese), Arabic
FIFA confederation: AFC (Asian Football Confederation)
Extra footie fact: The women's Aussie team are known as the Matildas. Fans selected the name in the 1990s from the song "Waltzing Matilda." (Losing names were Blue Flyers, Lorikeets, and Soccertoos.)

CANADA

Where in the world: North America
Capital city: Ottawa
Population: 38,794,813
What people speak: English, French, Chinese languages, Spanish
FIFA confederation: Concacaf (Confederation of North, Central America and Caribbean Association Football)
Extra footie fact: Canadian legend Christine Sinclair scored 190 goals since her first international game at age 16 in 2000. That's an all-time record for men or women. She retired from the national team in 2023 and club soccer in 2024.

CHINA

Where in the world: East Asia
Capital city: Beijing
Population: 1,416,043,270
What people speak: Standard Chinese or Mandarin, Yue (Cantonese), Wu (Shanghainese)
FIFA confederation: AFC (Asian Football Confederation)
Extra footie fact: The first official Women's World Cup took place in Guangdong, China, in 1991. Only twelve teams participated.

COLOMBIA

Where in the world: South America
Capital city: Bogotá
Population: 49,588,357
What people speak: Spanish, Indigenous languages
FIFA confederation: CONMEBOL (South American Football Confederation)
Extra footie fact: Linda Caicedo of Colombia struck a world-class goal in an upset victory over Germany at the 2023 Women's World Cup. Fans voted the 18-year-old's strike the best of the tournament.

COSTA RICA

Where in the world: Central America
Capital city: San José
Population: 5,265,575
What people speak: Spanish, English
FIFA confederation: Concacaf (Confederation of North, Central America and Caribbean Association Football)
Extra footie fact: Raquel "Rocky" Rodríguez notched Costa Rica's first-ever Women's World Cup goal against Spain in 2015. She still leads her closest teammate by nearly 40 goals.

DENMARK

Where in the world: Northern Europe
Capital city: Copenhagen
Population: 5,973,136
What people speak: Danish, Faroese, Greenlandic (Inuit dialect), English
FIFA confederation: UEFA (Union of European Football Associations)
Extra footie fact: In her first game with the Danish national team in 2009, Pernille Harder hit a hat trick. She was 16.

ENGLAND

Where in the world: Western Europe
Capital city: London
Population: 57,112,500
What people speak: English, Cornish
FIFA confederation: UEFA (Union of European Football Associations)
Extra footie fact: England reached their first Women's World Cup final in 2023, but it ended there, in a 1–0 loss to Spain. The United Kingdom was the sole bidder to host the 2035 Women's World Cup.

FRANCE

Where in the world: Western Europe
Capital city: Paris
Population: 68,374,591
What people speak: French, regional dialects and languages
FIFA confederation: UEFA (Union of European Football Associations)
Extra footie fact: France hosted the Women's World Cup once (in 2019). The team's best result was fourth place, in 2011.

GERMANY

Where in the world: Central Europe
Capital city: Berlin
Population: 84,119,100
What people speak: German, Danish, Frisian, Sorbian
FIFA confederation: UEFA (Union of European Football Associations)
Extra footie fact: Germany (and Spain) are the only countries to have won the men's and women's World Cups.

HAITI

Where in the world: In the Caribbean Sea (North America)
Capital city: Port-au-Prince
Population: 11,753,943
What people speak: French, Creole
FIFA confederation: Concacaf (Confederation of North, Central America and Caribbean Association Football)
Extra footie fact: Haiti made its first Women's World Cup appearance in 2023.

ITALY

Where in the world: Southern Europe
Capital city: Rome
Population: 60,964,931
What people speak: Italian, German, French, Slovene
FIFA confederation: UEFA (Union of European Football Associations)
Extra footie fact: The Italian women's soccer team, called La Azzurre, wear blue uniforms, a color not found on their flag. *Azzurro*, Italian for "blue," was the Italian royal family's official color.

JAMAICA

Where in the world: In the Caribbean Sea (North America)
Capital city: Kingston
Population: 2,823,713
What people speak: English, Jamaican patois
FIFA confederation: Concacaf (Confederation of North, Central America and Caribbean Association Football)
Extra footie fact: In 2019, Jamaica became the first Caribbean nation to qualify for the Women's World Cup.

JAPAN

Where in the world: East Asia
Capital city: Tokyo
Population: 123,201,945
What people speak: Japanese
FIFA confederation: AFC (Asian Football Confederation)
Extra footie fact: Japan made history as the first Asian country to win a Women's World Cup in 2011. They defeated the U.S. in a final that ended in a 5–2 penalty shootout.

MOROCCO

Where in the world: North Africa
Capital city: Rabat
Population: 37,387,585
What people speak: Arabic, Tamazight languages, French
FIFA confederation: CAF (Confederation of African Football)
Extra footie fact: In 2023, Morocco became the first Arab nation to compete in the Women's World Cup.

NETHERLANDS

Where in the world: Western Europe
Capital city: Amsterdam
Population: 17,772,378
What people speak: Dutch
FIFA confederation: UEFA (Union of European Football Associations)
Extra footie fact: Dutch star Vivianne Miedema was ruled out of the 2023 Women's World Cup due to injury. By then, she had already scored 95 goals in 115 international games.

NEW ZEALAND

Where in the world: Oceania
Capital city: Wellington
Population: 5,161,211
What people speak: English, Maori, Samoan, Northern Chinese
FIFA confederation: OFC (Oceania Football Confederation)
Extra footie fact: The Women's World Cup featured 32 teams for the first time in 2023. New Zealand, along with Australia, qualified automatically as host nations.

NIGERIA

Where in the world: West Africa
Capital city: Abuja
Population: 236,747,130
What people speak: English, Hausa, Yoruba, Igbo (Ibo)
FIFA confederation: CAF (Confederation of African Football)
Extra footie fact: Nigeria is the only African team to have participated in every Women's World Cup since the first in 1991.

NORWAY

Where in the world: Northern Europe
Capital city: Oslo
Population: 5,509,733
What people speak: Bokmal Norwegian, Nynorsk Norwegian, Sami
FIFA confederation: UEFA (Union of European Football Associations)
Extra footie fact: Norway is the smallest nation to win a Women's World Cup, in 1995.

PANAMA

Where in the world: Central America
Capital city: Panama City
Population: 4,470,241
What people speak: Spanish, Indigenous languages
FIFA confederation: Concacaf (Confederation of North, Central America and Caribbean Association Football)
Extra footie fact: Panama qualified for the Women's World Cup for the first time in 2023.

PHILIPPINES

Where in the world: Southeast Asia
Capital city: Manila
Population: 118,277,063
What people speak: Filipino (based on Tagalog), English
FIFA confederation: AFC (Asian Football Confederation)
Extra footie fact: In 2022, the Philippines women's team overcame Chinese Taipei in a thrilling penalty shootout to clinch a spot in their first World Cup (women's or men's).

PORTUGAL

Where in the world: Southern Europe
Capital city: Lisbon
Population: 10,207,177
What people speak: Portuguese, Mirandese
FIFA confederation: UEFA (Union of European Football Associations)
Extra footie fact: Portugal nearly eliminated the United States in its first Women's World Cup in 2023. In the final minutes, Ana Capeta fired a low shot that went off the goalpost—luckily for the U.S.

REPUBLIC OF IRELAND

Where in the world: Western Europe
Capital city: Dublin
Population: 5,233,461
What people speak: English, Irish (Gaelic or Gaeilge)
FIFA confederation: UEFA (Union of European Football Associations)
Extra footie fact: The Irish women's team, known as the Girls in Green, made their first Women's World Cup appearance in 2023.

SOUTH AFRICA

Where in the world: Southern Africa
Capital city: Cape Town
Population: 60,442,647
What people speak: isiZulu, isiXhosa, Afrikaans, Sepedi
FIFA confederation: CAF (Confederation of African Football)
Extra footie fact: South Africa reached the Round of 16 for the first time in 2023. They upset eighth-ranked Italy, 3–2, with a late goal.

SOUTH KOREA

Where in the world: East Asia
Capital city: Seoul
Population: 52,081,799
What people speak: Korean, English
FIFA confederation: AFC (Asian Football Confederation)
Extra footie fact: The youngest player in Women's World Cup history came on with just 12 minutes left in South Korea's 2023 opener against Colombia. Casey Yu-jin Phair was just 16 years and 26 days old.

SPAIN

Where in the world: Southern Europe
Capital city: Madrid
Population: 47,280,433
What people speak: Castilian Spanish, Catalan, Galician, Basque
FIFA confederation: UEFA (Union of European Football Associations)
Extra footie fact: Spain won its first Women's World Cup in 2023. It was Olga Carmona who scored the decisive goal in the final against England.

SWEDEN

Where in the world: Northern Europe
Capital city: Stockholm
Population: 10,589,835
What people speak: Swedish
FIFA confederation: UEFA (Union of European Football Associations)
Extra footie fact: Sweden has qualified for all nine Women's World Cups—along with Brazil, Germany, Japan, Nigeria, Norway, and United States.

SWITZERLAND

Where in the world: Western Europe
Capital city: Bern
Population: 8,860,574
What people speak: German, French, Italian, Romansh
FIFA confederation: UEFA (Union of European Football Associations)
Extra footie fact: Swiss forward Fabienne Humm stunned Ecuador in 2015 with the fastest hat trick in Women's World Cup history. She took just five minutes. (Her team went on to win, 10–1.)

UNITED STATES

Where in the world: North America
Capital city: Washington, D.C.
Population: 341,963,408
What people speak: English, Spanish, Hawaiian, other Indigenous languages
FIFA confederation: Concacaf (Confederation of North, Central America and Caribbean Association Football)
Extra footie fact: The most goals (5) scored by an individual in a Women's World Cup match was achieved by two Americans—Michelle Akers in 1991 and Alex Morgan in 2019.

VIETNAM

Where in the world: Southeast Asia
Capital city: Hà Noi
Population: 105,758,975
What people speak: Vietnamese, English, French, Chinese
FIFA confederation: AFC (Asian Football Confederation)
Extra footie fact: The women's team of Vietnam, known as the Golden Star Warriors, made their first Women's World Cup appearance in 2023.

ZAMBIA

Where in the world: Southern Africa
Capital city: Lusaka
Population: 20,799,116
What people speak: Bantu languages, English
FIFA confederation: CAF (Confederation of African Football)
Extra footie fact: Barbra Banda scored the 1,000th Women's World Cup goal in 2023. Her flawless penalty kick helped Zambia record its first-ever World Cup win (over Costa Rica).

33 TOUGH TRUTHS
ABOUT MAKING IT TO THE WORLD CUP

1. Training for the World Cup takes months—years, really—of intense preparation, focusing on fitness, tactics, and team chemistry.

2. Elite footballers train almost every day, with sessions that include running, strength work, technical drills, and team practices.

3. To perform at their best, players need eight hours of sleep.

4. They also require good nutrition, hydration, and treatment for muscle strain.

5. Professional soccer players can burn about 1,500 calories during a single match.

6. Recovery is just as important as training.

7. When teams are traveling, they do light exercises and recovery routines to prevent fatigue.

8. On match days, players arrive about three hours before kickoff.

9. After arriving at the stadium, they concentrate on mental preparation, do light warmups, and review strategy.

10. Footballers run, dribble, pass, challenge opponents, jump for headers, and slide tackle rivals, among many other skills.

11. During a match, a typical midfielder runs from 5 to 9 miles (8 to 14.5 km).

12. The fastest basketball players in the NBA don't run more than 3 miles (5 km) a game.

13. In NFL games (the other kind of football), players who cover the most ground run only about 1.3 miles (2 km).

14. A batter in Major League Baseball would need to circle the bases 15 times to travel a distance of more than 1 mile (1.6 km).

15. The fastest soccer players in the world reach speeds of up to 20 miles (32 km) per hour.

16. Ghana's Kamaldeen Sulemana clocked the 2022 World Cup's fastest sprint speeds.

17. Sulemana ran more than 22 miles (35 km) per hour, followed by Spain's Nico Williams, Germany's David Raum, and the U.S.'s Antonee Robinson.

18. Many players use meditation to manage stress and visualize success.

19. Slow, deep breathing promotes relaxation. It also lowers levels of the stress hormone called cortisol.

20. Egyptian forward Mohamed Salah refers to himself as a "yoga man." He has incorporated yoga poses into his training for years.

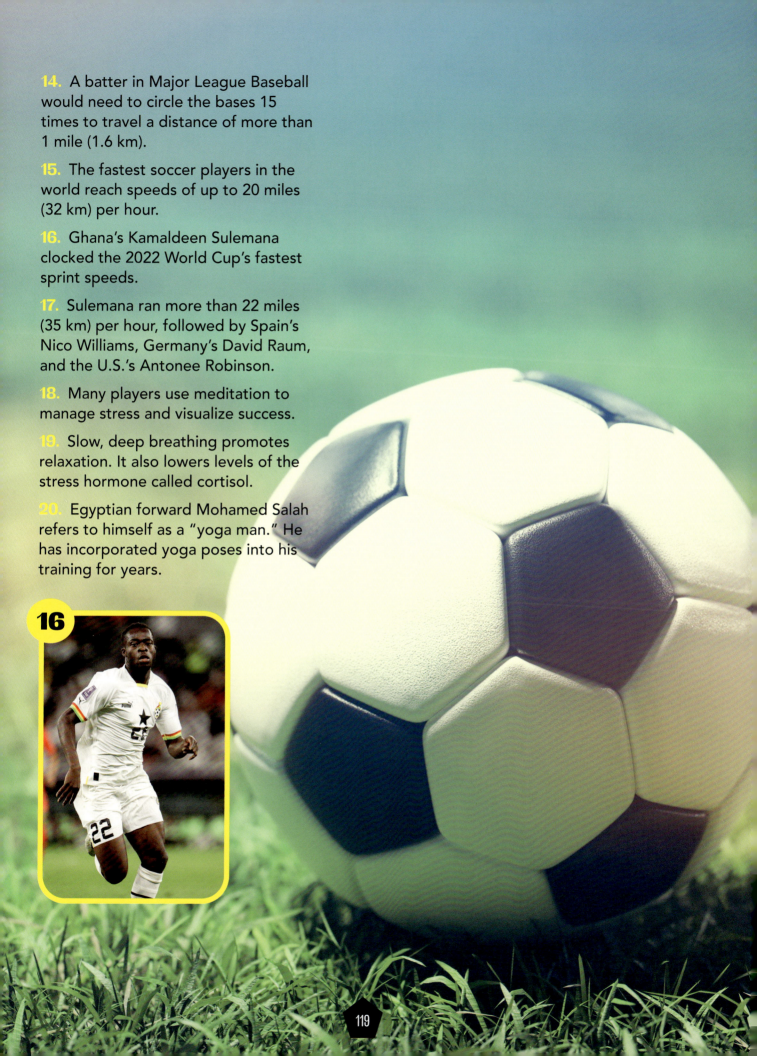

16

21. U.S. defender Naomi Girma practices a kind of meditation called mindfulness.

22. "When I'm facing big moments, I can put a lot of pressure on myself," Girma has said. "It's easy to worry about the next game or getting to the next round in a tournament. But the more I can stay in the moment and just focus on the next play, the better I do."

23. A six-week mindfulness program was shown to boost recovery and reduce stress for pro footballers.

24. The English men's national team has a breathing coach.

25. England players started using a deep breathing technique during penalty shootouts to stay focused and calm their nerves.

26. Elite players face immense pressure while competing for a spot on their country's World Cup roster.

27. In 2014, 32-year-old Landon Donovan, widely considered the best U.S. men's player, was cut from the World Cup team.

28. Alex Morgan, at almost 35 years old, was left off the U.S. women's roster just before the 2024 Olympics.

29. U.S. women's midfielder Sam Coffey, at 25, was not selected to play for the 2023 World Cup squad.

30. Unexpected omissions can be shocking to footballers and their fans, but it's just part of the game.

31. "I was looking forward to playing in Brazil, and as you can imagine, I am very disappointed with today's decision," Donovan shared. "I remain committed to helping grow soccer in the U.S. in the years to come."

32. "Today, I'm disappointed about not having the opportunity to represent our country on the Olympic stage," Morgan wrote on social media. "I look forward to supporting this team and cheering them on alongside the rest of our country."

33. At a press conference, Coffey later said: "It was an opportunity for me to learn a lot about myself." At the Olympics the following year, she was a star player and helped the team to win a gold medal.

27

GAME CHANGER
Alex Morgan

1. Alex Morgan was born in San Dimas, California, on July 2, 1989.

2. As a kid, Alex participated in various sports, including gymnastics. "When I went to soccer practice, I was really excited," Morgan said, "because I hadn't been there in four days."

3. The young striker earned her first cap and win in a friendly in Sandy, Utah, on March 31, 2010, the first snowy U.S. women's team match. The team celebrated the victory with snow angels.

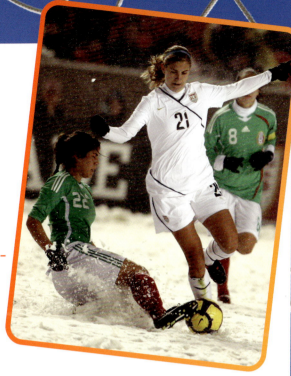

4. Morgan is a graduate of the University of California at Berkeley with a degree in political economy.

5. Western New York Flash selected Morgan in the 2011 Women's Professional Soccer draft. She was the first overall pick.

6. She wrote a best-selling children's book series that focuses on teamwork.

7. Morgan has been a successful advocate for equality, especially in terms of pay for women athletes.

8. This two-time World Cup champion and Olympic gold medalist scored 123 goals in 224 games for the U.S. national team.

9. Twice named the U.S. Soccer Female Player of the Year (2012 and 2018), Morgan was also a finalist for the FIFA Women's World Player of the Year in 2012, 2019, and 2022.

10. Alex Morgan announced her retirement in 2024.

24 AMERICAN PLAYERS TO WATCH
AND 24 EXTRA FOOTIE FACTS

There are always plenty of players—from veteran to rising star—in the mix to represent the U.S. national team at the next World Cups. Here are some footballers to keep an eye on.

1. TYLER ADAMS
Hometown: Wappingers Falls, New York
Born: February 14, 1999
Position: Midfielder
Years active: 2017–
Extra footie fact: After leading the U.S. to the 2022 World Cup knockout stages, Adams was named the 2022 U.S. Soccer Male Player of the Year.

2. FOLARIN BALOGUN
Hometown: New York, New York, and London, England
Born: July 3, 2001
Position: Forward
Years active: 2023–
Extra footie fact: Folarin Balogun, born in New York to Nigerian parents and raised in England, chose to play for the U.S. national team in 2023.

3. SAM COFFEY
Hometown: Sleepy Hollow, New York
Born: December 31, 1998
Position: Midfielder
Years active: 2022–
Extra footie fact: Before winning Olympic gold in 2024, this defensive midfielder helped the Portland Thorns win the 2022 NWSL Championship in her rookie year.

4. TIERNA DAVIDSON
Hometown: Menlo Park, California
Born: September 19, 1998
Position: Defender
Years active: 2018–
Extra footie fact: At 20, Tierna Davidson was the youngest member of the U.S. team that won the 2019 Women's World Cup.

5. SERGIÑO DEST
Hometown: Almere, Netherlands
Born: November 3, 2000
Position: Defender
Years active: 2019–
Extra footie fact: After choosing the U.S. over the Netherlands, Sergiño Dest became the first American to play—and score—for FC Barcelona in 2020.

8. NAOMI GIRMA
Hometown: San Jose, California
Born: June 14, 2000
Position: Defender
Years active: 2022–
Extra footie fact: This center back, the daughter of Ethiopian immigrants, was named to the Best FIFA Women's 11 in 2024.

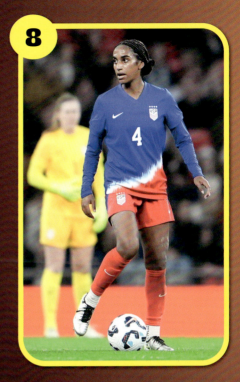

6. CRYSTAL DUNN
Hometown: Rockville Centre, New York
Born: July 3, 1992
Position: Defender/midfield/forward
Years active: 2013–
Extra footie fact: This versatile player for both club and country helped the team win the 2019 Women's World Cup and a gold medal at the 2024 Olympics.

7. EMILY FOX
Hometown: Ashburn, Virginia
Born: July 5, 1998
Position: Defender
Years active: 2018–
Extra footie fact: Emily Fox made her World Cup debut at the 2023 tournament, playing a key role in the team's defense.

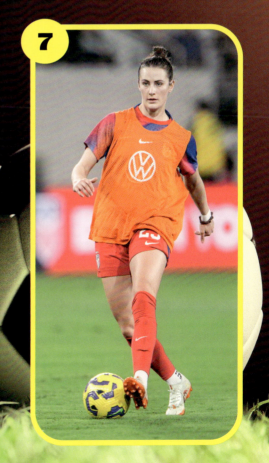

9. LINDSEY HEAPS
Hometown: Golden, Colorado
Born: May 26, 1994
Position: Midfielder
Years active: 2013–
Extra footie fact: Lindsey Heaps, formerly Horan, a 2019 Women's World Cup winner, was named to the Best FIFA Women's 11 in 2024.

10. ROSE LAVELLE
Hometown: Cincinnati, Ohio
Born: May 14, 1995
Position: Midfielder
Years active: 2017–
Extra footie fact: This creative playmaker scored the second goal in the final against the Netherlands to win the 2019 Women's World Cup.

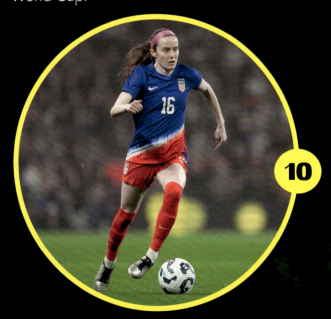

11. WESTON MCKENNIE
Hometown: Little Elm, Texas
Born: August 28, 1998
Position: Midfielder
Years active: 2017–
Extra footie fact: McKennie celebrates goals by waving his hand as if casting a spell with a wand, inspired by the Harry Potter books.

12. YUNUS MUSAH
Hometown: New York, New York, and London, England
Born: November 29, 2002
Position: Midfielder
Years active: 2020–
Extra footie fact: Born to Ghanaian parents and raised in Italy and England, this 2022 U.S. Soccer Young Male Player of the Year could have played for Ghana, Italy, or England.

13. CHRISTIAN PULISIC
Hometown: Hershey, Pennsylvania
Born: September 18, 1998
Position: Midfielder
Years active: 2016–
Extra footie fact: This U.S. star led the national team with a goal and two assists at the 2022 World Cup.

14. TIM REAM
Hometown: St. Louis, Missouri
Born: October 5, 1987
Position: Defender
Years active: 2010–
Extra footie fact: This reliable defender has captained the U.S. men's team and started in all four games at the 2022 World Cup.

15. GIO REYNA
Hometown: Bedford, New York
Born: November 13, 2002
Position: Midfielder
Years active: 2020–
Extra footie fact: At 18, Gio Reyna became the third-youngest scorer in team history, scoring against Panama in 2020. His father (Claudio Reyna) played on the senior U.S. national soccer team.

17. ANTONEE ROBINSON
Hometown: Liverpool, England
Born: August 8, 1997
Position: Defender
Years active: 2018–
Extra footie fact: This left back, a *Star Wars* fan, goes by the nickname Jedi, and said, "There's quite a bit of force in it." He was named the U.S. Soccer Male Player of the Year in 2024.

16. CHRIS RICHARDS
Hometown: Birmingham, Alabama
Born: March 28, 2000
Position: Defender
Years active: 2020–
Extra footie fact: Richards is considered one of the most promising young defenders in the U.S. national team pool.

18. TRINITY RODMAN
Hometown: Laguna Niguel, California
Born: May 20, 2002
Position: Forward
Years active: 2022–
Extra footie fact: Trinity Rodman, daughter of former NBA player Dennis Rodman, scored three goals and won a gold medal at the 2024 Olympics.

19. JAEDYN SHAW
Hometown: Frisco, Texas
Born: November 20, 2004
Position: Forward/midfielder
Years active: 2023–
Extra footie fact: Shaw, the team's first Vietnamese American, was the first player to score five goals in her first five starts.

20. MALLORY SWANSON
Hometown: Highlands Ranch, Colorado
Born: April 29, 1998
Position: Forward
Years active: 2016–
Extra footie fact: Swanson is a two-time Olympic gold medalist and a Women's World Cup champion. In the 2024 Olympics, she was the top U.S. scorer with four goals, including the only goal in the final.

21. ALYSSA THOMPSON
Hometown: Studio City, California
Born: November 7, 2004
Position: Forward
Years active: 2022–
Extra footie fact: Thompson, selected first in the 2023 NWSL Draft as a high schooler, made the 2023 Women's World Cup squad at age 18.

24. SOPHIA WILSON
Hometown: Windsor, Colorado
Born: August 10, 2000
Position: Forward
Years active: 2020–
Extra footie fact: Sophia Wilson, formerly Smith, scored two goals at the 2023 Women's World Cup and three goals at the 2024 Olympics.

22. MATT TURNER
Hometown: Park Ridge, New Jersey
Born: June 24, 1994
Position: Goalkeeper
Years active: 2021–
Extra footie fact: Turner was the starting U.S. goalkeeper in the 2022 World Cup and earned the Best Goalkeeper award in the 2023 Concacaf Nations League.

23. TIM WEAH
Hometown: Rosedale, New York
Born: February 22, 2000
Position: Forward
Years active: 2018–
Extra footie fact: This attacking forward recorded a 2022 World Cup goal and an assist. His father (George Weah) was the president of Liberia (2018–2024) and won the 1995 FIFA World Player of the Year and Ballon d'Or.

MEN'S WORLD CUP STARS

18 U.S. LEGENDS
AND 18 EXTRA FOOTIE FACTS

The U.S. men's team competed in the 1930, 1934, and 1950 World Cups—and every tournament since 1990 (except 2018). Here are some legendary footballers who helped shape U.S. soccer.

1. KELLYN ACOSTA
Hometown: Plano, Texas
Position: Midfielder
Appearances: 58
Goals: 2
Years active: 2016–2023
Extra footie fact: Kellyn Acosta was the first Japanese American footballer to represent the United States at the World Cup.

2. JOZY ALTIDORE
Hometown: Boca Raton, Florida
Position: Forward
Appearances: 115
Goals: 42
Years active: 2007–2019
Extra footie fact: With 42 goals for the U.S. national team, Altidore ranks third among all-time U.S. goal scorers, after Clint Dempsey and Landon Donovan.

3. DAMARCUS BEASLEY
Hometown: Fort Wayne, Indiana
Position: Midfielder/defender
Appearances: 126
Goals: 17
Years active: 2001–2017
Extra footie fact: DaMarcus Beasley is the only player in U.S. men's national team history to have appeared in four World Cups (2002, 2006, 2010, and 2014).

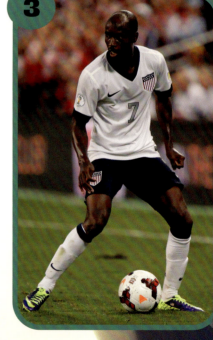

4. GREGG BERHALTER
Hometown: Tenafly, New Jersey
Position: Defender
Appearances: 44
Goals: 0
Years active: 1994–2006
Extra footie fact: Gregg Berhalter is the first American to play in the World Cup and later serve as the head coach of the U.S. men's national team.

5. MICHAEL BRADLEY
Hometown: Pennington, New Jersey
Position: Midfielder
Appearances: 151
Goals: 17
Years active: 2006–2019
Extra footie fact: This team captain, nicknamed the General by fans, played in the 2010 and 2014 World Cups. He retired with the third-most caps in U.S. men's national team history, after Cobi Jones and Landon Donovan.

6. JOHN BROOKS
Hometown: Berlin, Germany
Position: Defender
Appearances: 45
Goals: 3
Years active: 2013–2021
Extra footie fact: Brooks was the first substitute to score for the U.S. in World Cup history, netting the winner in the 86th minute against Ghana in 2014.

7. CLINT DEMPSEY
Hometown: Nacogdoches, Texas
Position: Forward
Appearances: 141
Goals: 57
Years active: 2004–2017
Extra footie fact: Soccer icon Clint Dempsey is the only U.S. man to have scored in three different World Cups (2006, 2010, and 2014).

8. LANDON DONOVAN
Hometown: Redlands, California
Position: Forward
Appearances: 157
Goals: 57
Years active: 2000–2014
Extra footie fact: This soccer legend retired as the U.S. men's national team's all-time top scorer with 57 goals, a record Clint Dempsey matched in 2017. As of early 2025, Donovan was also tied with Lionel Messi for most assists (58) in international football history.

9. BRAD FRIEDEL
Hometown: Lakewood, Ohio
Position: Goalkeeper
Appearances: 82
Clean sheets: 24
Years active: 1992–2004
Extra footie fact: Friedel, nicknamed the Human Wall, saved two PKs at the 2002 World Cup—one in a draw with South Korea and another in a 3–2 win over Portugal—helping the U.S. reach the quarterfinals.

10. TIM HOWARD
Hometown: North Brunswick, NJ
Position: Goalkeeper
Appearances: 121
Clean sheets: 42
Years active: 2002–2017
Extra footie fact: Tim Howard earned the most caps of any U.S. keeper in men's national team history. In a U.S. loss to Belgium at the 2014 World Cup, he set a tournament record for the most saves in a single match—16.

11. COBI JONES
Hometown: Westlake Village, California
Position: Midfielder
Appearances: 164
Goals: 15
Years active: 1992–2004
Extra footie fact: Jones (13), the all-time leader in caps for the U.S. men's national team, played in three World Cups (1994, 1998, and 2002).

12. JERMAINE JONES
Hometown: Frankfurt, Germany
Position: Midfielder
Appearances: 69
Goals: 4
Years active: 2010–2017
Extra footie fact: This German-U.S. citizen scored the equalizing goal against Portugal in the 2014 World Cup.

13. KASEY KELLER
Hometown: Lacey, Washington
Position: Goalkeeper
Appearances: 102
Clean sheets: 47
Years active: 1990–2007
Extra footie fact: Keller, who started every match at the 2006 World Cup, holds the record for most shutouts by a U.S. men's national team goalkeeper. He was named U.S. Soccer Male Player of the Year in 1997, 1999, and 2005.

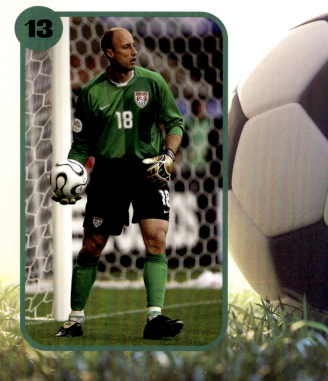

14. ALEXI LALAS
Hometown: Birmingham, Michigan
Position: Defender
Appearances: 96
Goals: 10
Years active: 1991–1998
Extra footie fact: Alexi Lalas made a name for himself as a defender at the 1994 World Cup. Fans watch him now as a TV soccer analyst.

15. TONY MEOLA
Hometown: Belleville, New Jersey
Position: Goalkeeper
Appearances: 100
Clean sheets: 32
Years active: 1988–2006
Extra footie fact: Meola, the starting goalkeeper from 1990 to 1994, helped lead the U.S. to the knockout stages of the 1994 World Cup.

16. CLAUDIO REYNA
Hometown: Livingston, New Jersey
Position: Midfielder
Appearances: 112
Goals: 8
Years active: 1994–2006
Extra footie fact: Claudio Reyna, father of active U.S. men's player Gio Reyna, made four different World Cup rosters, captaining the 2002 and 2006 squads.

17. ERIC WYNALDA
Hometown: Westlake Village, California
Position: Forward
Appearances: 106
Goals: 34
Years active: 1990–2000
Extra footie fact: Eric Wynalda played in three World Cups (1990, 1994, and 1998). His free kick in the 1994 World Cup match against Switzerland helped the U.S. advance.

18. DEANDRE YEDLIN
Hometown: Seattle, Washington
Position: Defender
Appearances: 81
Goals: 0
Years active: 2014–2023
Extra footie fact: The 2022 U.S. squad featured just one player with previous World Cup experience: Yedlin, who had competed in 2014.

11 GOLDEN BALLS:
BEST MEN'S WORLD CUP PLAYERS

The Golden Ball has been awarded to the best player at each men's World Cup tournament since 1982. That player is officially selected by the FIFA Technical Study Group—a panel of experts who analyze and evaluate player performances. Second- and third-place finishers win the Silver Ball and the Bronze Ball. But gold is best, naturally. Goalkeepers may win the Golden Ball. In fact, Oliver Kahn did it in 2002.

Year	Player	Nation
2022	Lionel Messi	Argentina
2018	Luka Modric	Croatia
2014	Lionel Messi	Argentina
2010	Diego Forlán	Uruguay
2006	Zinedine Zidane	France
2002	Oliver Kahn	Germany
1998	Ronaldo	Brazil
1994	Romário	Brazil
1990	Salvatore Schillaci	Italy
1986	Diego Maradona	Argentina
1982	Paolo Rossi	Italy

GAME CHANGER
Johan Cruyff

1. Hendrik Johannes Cruijff, known as Johan Cruyff, was born in 1947 in Amsterdam, Netherlands.

2. After joining Amsterdam's Ajax soccer youth academy as a 10-year-old, Johan made his senior team debut at 17.

3. Reflecting on soccer, Johan Cruyff once said, "Football is a game of mistakes. Whoever makes the fewest mistakes wins."

4. The serious Dutch forward didn't make many mistakes, winning six league titles, four national cups, and three European cups with Ajax.

5. He also won the Ballon d'Or in 1971, 1973, and 1974.

6. Cruyff led the Netherlands to the 1974 World Cup final, where they were defeated by West Germany.

7. Although Cruyff never won the official Golden Ball, which was introduced in 1982, he proved himself at the 1974 tournament.

8. Johan Cruyff helped promote the style of play called *totaalvoetbal* ("total football").

9. Total football, created by Dutch coach Rinus Michels, encourages players to shift positions and move freely on the field. The style focuses on quick passes, possession of the ball, and aggressive defense.

10. After retiring from play, Cruyff became an influential coach. He died in 2016.

28 GOLDEN BOOTS: TOP SCORERS AT EVERY MEN'S WORLD CUP

The Golden Boot, given to the top scorer, was called the Golden Shoe from 1982 to 2006. The 1994 winners were tied. Since then, ties have been broken by most assists and fewest minutes played per goal. The top scorers from 1930 to 1978 are also listed, though there was no official award.

Year	Winner	Nation	Goals
2022	Kylian Mbappé	France	8
2018	Harry Kane	England	6
2014	James Rodríguez	Colombia	6
2010	Thomas Müller	Germany	5
2006	Miroslav Klose	Germany	5
2002	Ronaldo	Brazil	8
1998	Davor Suker	Croatia	6
1994	Oleg Salenko	Russia	6
	Hristo Stoichkov	Bulgaria	
1990	Salvatore Schillaci	Italy	6
1986	Gary Lineker	England	6
1982	Paolo Rossi	Italy	6
1978	Mario Kempes	Argentina	6
1974	Grzegorz Lato	Poland	7
1970	Gerd Müller	Germany	10
1966	Eusébio	Portugal	9
1962	Flórián Albert	Hungary	4
	Valentin Ivanov	Soviet Union	
	Garrincha	Brazil	
	Vavá	Brazil	
	Drazan Jerkovic	Yugoslavia	
	Leonel Sánchez	Chile	
1958	Just Fontaine	France	13
1954	Sándor Kocsis	Hungary	11
1950	Ademir	Brazil	9
1938	Leônidas	Brazil	7
1934	Oldrich Nejedly	Czechoslovakia	5
1930	Guillermo Stábile	Argentina	8

GAME CHANGER
Harry Kane

1. English striker Harry Kane has scored over 400 goals for club and country.

2. His legendary goal-scoring ability earned him the Golden Boot at the 2018 World Cup in Russia.

3. "When you get a clear sight of goal, aim low and hard across the goalkeeper," Kane said. "These are the most difficult shots to save."

4. Harry Kane, born in 1993 in East London, England, grew up just 15 minutes from the Tottenham Hotspur football stadium.

5. Young Harry attended the same school and played for the same youth club as David Beckham once had.

6. Harry signed his first contract with Tottenham Hotspur on his 16th birthday in 2009. From 2010 to 2023, he scored 280 goals for the team.

7. Kane has won the Premier League Golden Boot three times—in the 2015, 2016, and 2020 seasons.

8. After debuting for the English senior team in 2015, Harry Kane, at just 21 years old, established himself as a key player.

9. In 2023, Kane became the English men's all-time leading scorer after converting a penalty in a Euro qualifier against Italy. Wayne Rooney ranks second with 53 goals.

10. Kane is a fan of American football and even named two family puppies after quarterbacks Tom Brady and Russell Wilson.

8 WINNERS OF THE GOLDEN GLOVE: BEST MEN'S WORLD CUP KEEPERS

The best goalkeeper at each World Cup is awarded the Golden Glove. The selection is made by the FIFA Technical Study Group. For the men's World Cup tournament, the honor was known as the Lev Yashin Award from 1994 to 2006. It was named after the Russian goalkeeper.

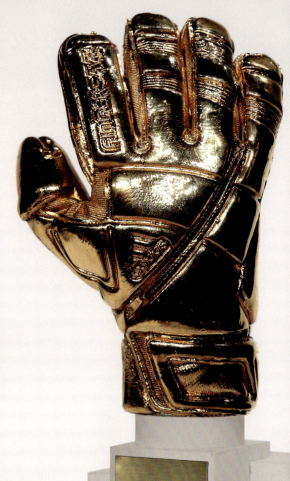

Year	Winner	Nation	Clean Sheet
2022	Emiliano Martínez	Argentina	3
2018	Thibaut Courtois	Belgium	3
2014	Manuel Neuer	Germany	4
2010	Iker Casillas	Spain	5
2006	Gianluigi Buffon	Italy	5
2002	Oliver Kahn	Germany	5
1998	Fabien Barthez	France	5
1994	Michel Preud'homme	Belgium	2

GAME CHANGER
Lev Yashin

1. In 1963, Lev Yashin became the first and only goalkeeper to win the Ballon d'Or.

2. Yashin revolutionized goalkeeping with bold saves, punches, quick throws, and control of the penalty area.

3. Over his career, Yashin recorded 207 clean sheets and stopped more than 150 penalty kicks.

4. Lev Yashin was born in 1929 in Moscow, Russia. His first name means "lion" in Russian.

5. Lev fled the Nazis during World War II with his family, and worked in a weapons factory at age 13.

6. After returning to Moscow, Lev joined the Dynamo club, where he played ice hockey and soccer.

7. From 1954 to 1970, Yashin played in goal for Dynamo, winning five Soviet league titles and three Soviet cups in football.

8. The Soviet national team, with Yashin in net, earned a gold medal at the 1956 Olympics, the 1960 European Nations' Cup, and a fourth-place finish at the 1966 World Cup.

9. Yashin struggled with ill health and passed away at age 60 in 1990.

10. Lev Yashin appeared in black uniform and cap on the official 2018 FIFA World Cup poster, making a save. His nickname was the Black Spider.

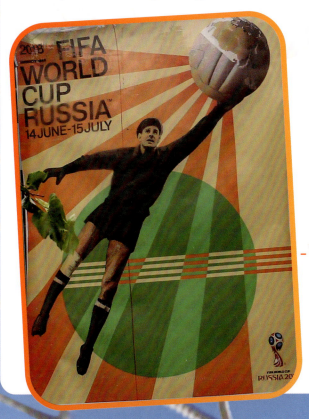

17 WINNERS OF THE MEN'S FIFA YOUNG PLAYER AWARD

The FIFA Technical Study Group selects the winner of the FIFA World Cup Young Player Award. The honor was called the Best Young Player Award in 2006 and 2010. Winners must be 21 years old or younger. The public chose the men's winners from 1958 to 2002 in an online FIFA survey in 2009.

Year	Winner	Nation	Age	Position
2022	Enzo Fernández	Argentina	21	Midfielder
2018	Kylian Mbappé	France	19	Forward
2014	Paul Pogba	France	21	Midfielder
2010	Thomas Müller	Germany	20	Midfielder/forward
2006	Lukas Podolski	Germany	21	Midfielder/forward
2002	Landon Donovan	U.S.	20	Midfielder/forward
1998	Michael Owen	England	18	Forward
1994	Marc Overmars	Netherlands	21	Midfielder
1990	Robert Prosinecki	Yugoslavia	21	Midfielder
1986	Enzo Scifo	Belgium	20	Midfielder
1982	Manuel Amoros	France	21	Defender
1978	Antonio Cabrini	Italy	20	Defender
1974	Wladyslaw Zmuda	Poland	20	Defender
1970	Teófilo Cubillas	Peru	21	Midfielder
1966	Franz Beckenbauer	West Germany	20	Defender
1962	Flórián Albert	Hungary	20	Forward
1958	Pelé	Brazil	17	Forward

WHO MIGHT BE NEXT?
43 RISING MEN'S STARS FROM AROUND THE WORLD

Here are some football talents (most born in 2003 or after) who could shine at the next World Cups.

1. **Noah Atubolu**, a German goalkeeper of Igbo Nigerian descent, has quick reflexes and ball distribution often compared to a young Manuel Neuer. He played his first senior team game for Bundesliga club SC Freiburg in 2023.

2. **Carlos Noom Quomah Baleba**, the son of a pro footballer, has played in the midfield for the Cameroon national team since 2024. His professional career started in Lille, France.

3. **Roony Bardghji**, a Swedish player born in Kuwait to Syrian parents, has been called a tricky left-footed winger. He started his professional career in Copenhagen, Denmark, appearing in his first game at age 16.

4. English midfielder **Jude Bellingham** scored a goal in the 2022 World Cup against Iran at age 19. He was named to the prestigious Best FIFA Men's 11 in 2024.

5. **Eliesse Ben Seghir**, born in France, has represented the Morocco national team since 2024 as a left winger.

6. Swedish midfielder **Lucas Bergvall** made his first appearance for the senior national team in 2024 at age 19. He debuted for Tottenham Hotspur the same year.

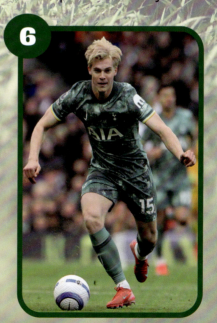

7. At 19, forward **Cade Cowell** of Ceres, California, scored his first international goal for the men's senior U.S. team against Trinidad and Tobago at the 2023 Concacaf Gold Cup.

8. **Pau Cubarsí**, a center back, represents Spain and speaks only Catalan.

9. Winger **Amara Diouf**, at age 15, became the youngest member of Senegal's senior national team in 2023.

10. **Désiré Doué** played five matches for France at the 2024 Olympics, helping the team win a silver medal.

11. **Jhon Durán** has been a forward on the Colombian national team since 2022. The next year, at 19, he scored his first international goal in a friendly victory over Japan.

12. **Claudio Echeverri** of Argentina is nicknamed El Diablito (Spanish for "the Little Devil"). The attacking midfielder started his professional football career in 2023 at a Buenos Aires club at age 17. He moved to Manchester City the next year.

13. Midfielder **Bilal El Khannouss** earned his first senior cap for Morocco in the 2022 World Cup third-place playoff against Croatia. He was born in Belgium.

14. **Endrick** is a forward from Brazil. He scored three goals for his national team in 2024.

15. **Estêvão**, at 17, became the fifth-youngest player to wear the Brazil jersey in 2024.

16. **Adrian Gill**, a midfielder born in Denver, Colorado, grew up in Spain and plays professionally for Barcelona but chose not to play for the Spanish national team.

17. **Luis Guilherme**, an attacking midfielder from Brazil, has recorded a top running speed of 22.6 miles (36.4 km) per hour. After playing pro soccer in Brazil, he debuted for West Ham United at age 18 in 2024.

20. **Diego Kochen**, an American goalkeeper eligible to play for Peru or Venezuela through his parents, was first called up to the U.S. national team in 2024. He was raised in Florida and Spain. Kochen once said after a game: "I wasn't paying attention to the badge on the opponents' jersey. I was only focusing on what was in front of me. But this was a challenge to test ourselves against great competition." His age at the time? 11.

21. Defender **Rico Lewis** earned his first cap for England's senior team the day before his 19th birthday.

18. **Arda Güler** is a left-footed attacking midfielder. Dubbed the Turkish Messi for his dribbling and passing skills, he notched his first goal for the senior national team at 18 in 2023.

22. **Kobbie Mainoo**, a midfielder, earned 10 caps for England in 2024. Marcus Rashford, one of his teammates, described Mainoo as composed and confident: "Nothing seems to faze him."

19. **Jorrel Hato**, a defender from the Netherlands, subbed for captain Virgil van Dijk in a UEFA Euro qualifying match in 2023. "I'm not afraid to make mistakes," he said.

23. **Lewis Miley**, born in Stanley, England, is a central midfielder.

24. **Gabriel Moscardo** is a Brazilian defensive midfielder.

25. **Jamal Musiala** stood out for Germany at the 2022 World Cup, with 12 dribbles against Costa Rica—the most for a teenager in tournament history.

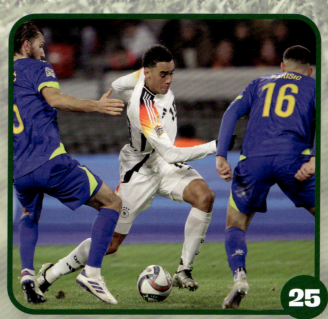

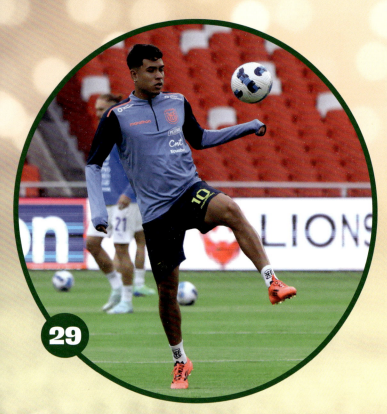

29

31. **Ricardo Pepi**, a forward from Texas, was named both the U.S. Soccer Young Male Player of the Year and the MLS Young Player of the Year in 2021.

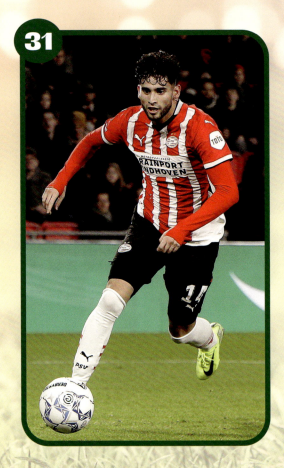

31

26. **Ethan Nwaneri** became the youngest player to appear in the Premier League in 2022. The English midfielder, age 15, came off the bench for Arsenal.

27. Two-footed **Antonio Nusa** scored in his first match on Norway's senior team in a friendly against Jordan in 2023.

28. **Assan Ouédraogo** is a midfielder from Germany. His father, a former international footballer from Burkina Faso, scored seven goals for his country.

29. **Kendry Páez**, a midfielder from Guayaquil, Ecuador, plays professionally in his country. In 2023, at age 16, he became the youngest player to score in a CONMEBOL World Cup qualifier.

30. Midfielder **Kevin Paredes** was named the 2023 U.S. Soccer Young Male Player of the Year. He earned his first cap for the U.S. national team the same year. His two goals against Guinea at the 2024 Olympics helped the U.S. advance to the quarterfinals.

32. **Guillaume Restes** was the starting goalkeeper for the French Olympic team in 2024, helping them win the silver medal.

33. **Vitor Roque**, a striker, has already been capped at the senior level by Brazil. Teammate Vinícius Júnior is one of his inspirations.

34. **Xavi Simons**, a midfielder, has played on the national team for the Netherlands since 2022. He scored three goals for his country in 2024.

35. American **Pedro Soma**, born in Boca Raton, Florida, to a Brazilian mother and an American father, relocated to Barcelona in 2018. He is a midfielder.

41. **Kenan Yildiz**, born in Regensburg, Germany, is eligible to play for Turkey through his father. The midfielder scored his first goal for the Turkey national team in 2023.

42. **Leny Yoro**, a center back, was called up for the 2024 French Olympic team but couldn't play because of club duties. He could also play for Côte d'Ivoire through his father.

43. **Warren Zaïre-Emery**, French midfielder, scored in his first senior appearance in 2023, becoming the team's second-youngest goal scorer at 17. He has been compared to Jude Bellingham.

36. **Cavan Sullivan** is a left-footed midfielder from Norristown, Pennsylvania. He signed with Philadelphia Union in 2024 at age 14, becoming the youngest player in the MLS. In 2025, Sullivan said, "At the end of the day, I want to win a World Cup, win a Champions League, win a Premier League, and live up to my potential."

37. **Mathys Tel**, a striker from France, is known for his speed and dribbling.

38. Midfielder **Arthur Vermeeren** made his national team debut for Belgium in 2023.

39. **Florian Wirtz** is a serious German talent, having scored six goals for the national team in 2024.

40. **Lamine Yamal**, son of a Moroccan father and an Equatorial Guinean mother, is a left-footed right winger. In 2023, the Spanish 16-year-old became the youngest-ever scorer at the UEFA Euro 2024. He earned a spot on the 2024 Best FIFA Men's 11.

WOMEN'S WORLD CUP STARS

18 U.S. LEGENDS
AND 18 EXTRA FOOTIE FACTS

The U.S. women's team triumphed in the 1991, 1999, 2015, and 2019 Women's World Cups. Here are some legendary game changers in U.S. soccer.

1. MICHELLE AKERS
Hometown: Shoreline, California
Position: Forward/midfield
Appearances: 153
Goals: 105
Years active: 1985–2000
Extra footie fact: This soccer pioneer scored the first official U.S. women's national team goal in a 1985 match against Denmark.

2. BRANDI CHASTAIN
Hometown: San Jose, California
Position: Forward/defender
Appearances: 192
Goals: 30
Years active: 1988–2004
Extra footie fact: In the the 1999 Women's World Cup final, Brandi Chastain took her penalty with her left foot, despite being right-footed. The coach suggested the strategy to outsmart the goalkeeper.

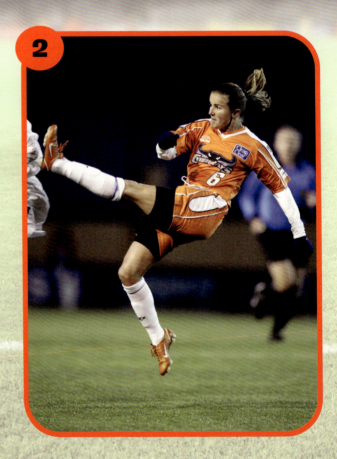

Extra footie fact: Hamm won two Olympic gold medals (1996 and 2004) and two World Cups (1991 and 1999). This soccer legend holds the record for the second-most goals (158) and the most assists (147) of any American, male or female.

6. LAUREN HOLIDAY
Hometown: Indianapolis, Indiana
Appearances: 133
Position: Midfielder
Goals: 24
Years active: 2007–2015
Extra footie fact: Lauren Holiday, formerly Cheney, is a 2015 Women's World Cup champion and two-time Olympic gold medalist. She runs a nonprofit that supports Black-owned businesses with her husband, NBA star Jrue Holiday.

3. JULIE ERTZ
Hometown: Mesa, Arizona
Position: Midfielder/defender
Appearances: 123
Goals: 20
Years active: 2013–2023
Extra footie fact: Julie Ertz, formerly Johnston, played a key role in the U.S. victories at the Women's World Cups in 2015 and 2019. In 2023, she returned to play every minute of the Women's World Cup alongside Naomi Girma on the back line.

7. ALI KRIEGER
Hometown: Dumfries, Virginia
Position: Defender
Appearances: 108
Goals: 1
Years active: 2008–2021
Extra footie fact: This two-time World Cup champion started every game for the U.S. national team in both the 2011 and 2015 tournaments. Krieger scored the decisive penalty kick in the quarterfinal shootout victory over Brazil at the 2011 Women's World Cup.

4. JULIE FOUDY
Hometown: Mission Viejo, California
Appearances: 274
Position: Midfielder
Goals: 45
Years active: 1988–2004
Extra footie fact: Foudy, a two-time World Cup champion and former team captain, received the FIFA Fair Play Award in 1998 for fighting child labor in sports manufacturing.

5. MIA HAMM
Hometown: Selma, Alabama
Position: Forward
Appearances: 276
Goals: 158
Years active: 1987–2004

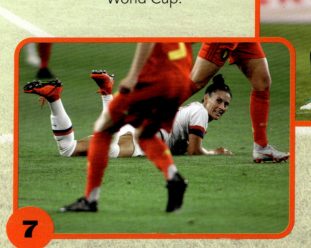

8. KRISTINE LILLY
Hometown: Wilton, Connecticut
Position: Midfielder
Appearances: 354
Goals: 130
Years active: 1987–2010
Extra footie fact: Kristine Lilly has more caps (354) and more World Cup games (30) than any other soccer player, man or woman. Lilly played in five Women's World Cups, winning in 1991 and 1999.

9. CARLI LLOYD
Hometown: Delran, New Jersey
Position: Midfielder/forward
Appearances: 316
Goals: 134
Years active: 2005–2021
Extra footie fact: Carli Lloyd, a winner of two Women's World Cups and two Olympic golds, earned the second-most caps in U.S. women's national team history, after Kristine Lilly.

10. ALEX MORGAN
Hometown: Diamond Bar, California
Position: Forward
Appearances: 224
Goals: 123
Years active: 2010–2024
Extra footie fact: A two-time Women's World Cup champion (2015 and 2019) and a 2012 Olympic gold medalist, Morgan is considered one of the best strikers in the history of U.S. women's soccer.

11. ALYSSA NAEHER
Hometown: Stratford, Connecticut
Position: Goalkeeper
Appearances: 115
Clean sheets: 69
Years active: 2014–2024
Extra footie fact: Alyssa Naeher is the only goalkeeper in women's soccer history to earn a shutout in both a World Cup final, in 2019, and an Olympic gold-medal game, in 2024. She was named the Best FIFA Women's Goalkeeper in 2024.

12. HEATHER O'REILLY
Hometown: East Brunswick, New Jersey
Position: Midfielder
Appearances: 231
Goals: 47
Years active: 2002–2016
Extra footie fact: Heather O'Reilly joined the women's national team as a high schooler. She retired in 2016 with one World Cup (2015) and three Olympic gold medals (2004, 2008, and 2012).

13. CHRISTINE PEARCE
Hometown: Fort Lauderdale, Florida
Position: Defender
Appearances: 311
Goals: 4
Years active: 1987–2015
Extra footie fact: Christine Pearce, formerly Rampone, retired with two World Cup titles and three Olympic gold medals. She played in five World Cup finals and four Olympic tournaments, securing a top-three finish in every one.

14. MEGAN RAPINOE
Hometown: Redding, California
Position: Midfielder
Appearances: 203
Goals: 63
Years active: 2006–2023
Extra footie fact: Rapinoe's 73 international assists rank third in U.S. women's national team history. Her most memorable assist was a long pass to Abby Wambach to even the score in the 122nd minute of quarterfinal against Brazil at the 2011 Women's World Cup, leading to a penalty shootout win.

15. BECKY SAUERBRUNN
Hometown: St. Louis, Missouri
Position: Defender
Appearances: 219
Goals: 0
Years active: 2008–2024
Extra footie fact: From 2013 to 2024, this center back started in 167 of 182 games, contributing to U.S. victories at the Women's World Cup in 2015 and 2019.

16. BRIANA SCURRY
Hometown: Dayton, Minnesota
Position: Goalkeeper
Appearances: 175
Clean sheets: 72
Years active: 1994–2008
Extra footie fact: When Briana Scurry was 12, she played in goal on a boys' team because there were no local girls' soccer leagues. She went on to start for the U.S. women's national team from 1995 to 2006, winning a World Cup title and two Olympic gold medals.

17. HOPE SOLO
Hometown: Richland, Washington
Position: Goalkeeper
Appearances: 202
Clean sheets: 102
Years active: 2000–2016
Extra footie fact: In 2016, Hope Solo became the first goalkeeper to record 100 shutouts in international competition. A World Cup champion and two-time Olympic gold medalist, she ranks as one the world's top keepers.

18. ABBY WAMBACH
Hometown: Rochester, New York
Position: Forward
Appearances: 255
Goals: 184
Years active: 2001–2015
Extra footie fact: Soccer icon Wambach competed in four Women's World Cups and won the 2015 tournament. Abby Wambach also held the record for the most international goals (184) scored by any player, male or female, until Christine Sinclair broke it in 2021. Wambach's stoppage-time header in the 2011 Women's World Cup quarterfinal against Brazil is considered one of the tournament's best ever.

9 GOLDEN BALLS
BEST WOMEN'S WORLD CUP PLAYERS

The Golden Ball has gone to the best player at each Women's World Cup since 1991. That player is officially selected by the FIFA Technical Study Group. The runners-up win the Silver Ball and the Bronze Ball.

Year	Winner	Nation
2023	Aitana Bonmatí	Spain
2019	Megan Rapinoe	U.S.
2015	Carli Lloyd	U.S.
2011	Homare Sawa	Japan
2007	Marta	Brazil
2003	Birgit Prinz	Germany
1999	Sun Wen	China
1995	Hege Riise	Norway
1991	Carin Jennings	U.S.

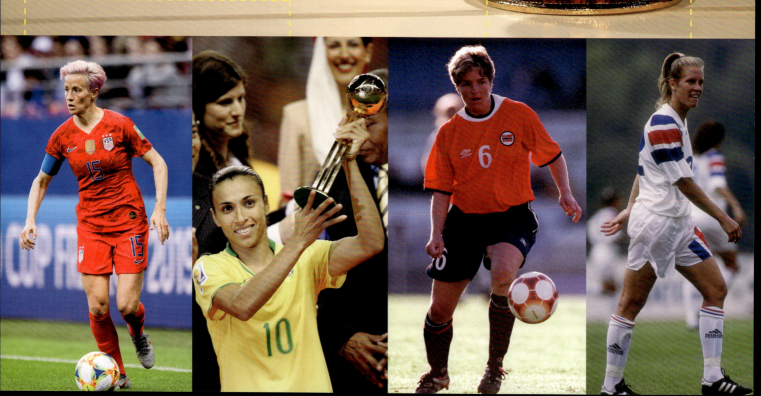

GAME CHANGER
Aitana Bonmatí

1. Aitana Bonmatí was born in 1998 in Catalonia, in northeastern Spain.

2. She speaks Catalan, Spanish, and English.

3. Bonmatí is her mother's last name. Her parents, both teachers, fought a Spanish law requiring a child's first surname be the father's. Bonmatí said, "This willingness to fight for women's rights, I feel I have that in my blood."

4. As a kid, Aitana admired FC Barcelona and its tiki-taka style, with short, quick passes to create spaces and move the ball forward.

5. At seven, Aitana began playing soccer and basketball with the boys at school.

6. After joining FC Barcelona's youth team at age 14, she was promoted to the first team the next season.

7. The midfielder stands just under 5 feet 4 inches (160 cm) tall. "Everything has its pros and cons," Bonmatí said. "I know that I'm going to win few balls in the air, but I'm more dynamic and faster than other teammates."

8. In 2023, Bonmatí led her country to its first Women's World Cup victory and received the Golden Ball as the best player.

9. She was awarded both the Best FIFA Women's Player of the Year and the Ballon d'Or Féminin in 2023 and in 2024.

10. Football manager Pep Guardiola, the architect of tiki-taka, called Aitana Bonmatí "the greatest female soccer player in the world."

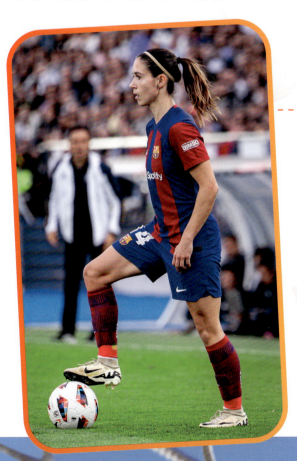

10 GOLDEN BOOTS: TOP SCORERS AT EVERY WOMEN'S WORLD CUP

The top scorer at each Women's World Cup wins the Golden Boot. At the 1991 Women's World Cup, the honor was called the Golden Shoe. In the case of ties, the Golden Boot goes to the player with the most assists and fewest minutes played per goal wins.

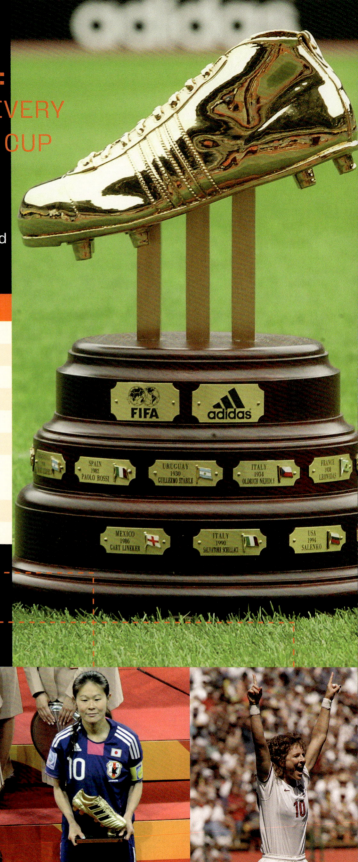

Year	Winner	Nation	Goals
2023	Hinata Miyazawa	Japan	5
2019	Megan Rapinoe	U.S.	6
2015	Célia Sasic	Germany	6
2011	Homare Sawa	Japan	5
2007	Marta	Brazil	7
2003	Birgit Prinz	Germany	7
1999	Sun Wen	China	7
	Sissi	Brazil	
1995	Ann Kristin Aarones	Norway	6
1991	Michelle Akers	U.S.	10

GAME CHANGER
Megan Rapinoe

1. Megan Rapinoe delivered clutch performances on the pitch until her retirement in 2023.

2. Known for her dynamic, creative play, she once said, "I play a certain style. I'm not willing to compromise that part of me."

3. The tactical midfielder earned two Women's World Cup titles, in 2015 and 2019, and a gold medal at the 2012 Olympics in London.

4. Rapinoe grew up in a small town near Redding, California, where she was born in 1985.

5. Megan and her twin sister first kicked soccer balls around the backyard together. At five, they tagged along to their brother's soccer practices until they were invited to join the under-eight boys' team.

6. Rapinoe played soccer at Oregon's University of Portland and then on professional teams in Chicago, Seattle, and France and on the U.S. national team.

7. At the 2019 Women's World Cup, Rapinoe received the Golden Boot for most goals and the Golden Ball as best player.

8. In 2019, she was named the Best FIFA Women's Player of the Year—and became the only American to win the Ballon d'Or Féminin.

9. Megan Rapinoe has championed racial justice, LGBTQ rights, and equal pay for women athletes.

10. Rapinoe was awarded the Presidential Medal of Freedom in 2022 for her leadership on and off the field. She was the first soccer player to earn the honor.

7 WINNERS OF THE GOLDEN GLOVE:
BEST WOMEN'S WORLD CUP KEEPERS

The best goalkeeper at each Women's World Cup is awarded the Golden Glove. The FIFA Technical Study Group makes the selection. For the Women's World Cup from 1999 to 2007, the honor was called a Best Goalkeeper Award. No official Golden Glove was given at the 1991 and 1995 tournaments.

Year	Winner	Nation	Clean Sheets
2023	Mary Earps	England	3
2019	Sari van Veenendaal	Netherlands	3
2015	Hope Solo	U.S.	5
2011	Hope Solo	U.S.	2
2007	Nadine Angerer	Germany	6
2003	Silke Rottenberg	Germany	2
1999	Gao Hong	China	4
	Briana Scurry	U.S.	

GAME CHANGER
Mary Earps

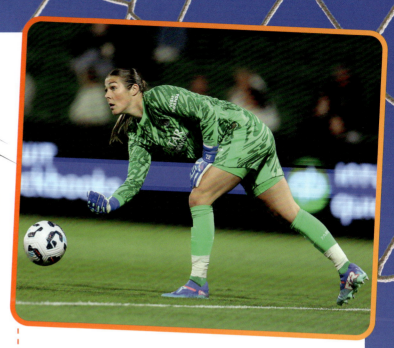

1. The first women's footballer honored with a wax figure at Madame Tussauds London was English goalkeeper Mary Earps. She won in a public vote of Lioness fans in 2024.

2. "This is not about me," Earps said. "This is a representation of how women's football has grown."

3. Her quick decision-making, reflexes, and distribution skills have earned Earps widespread praise.

4. Earps credits her flexibility in goal to learning dance as a child: "Ballet, tap, modern, and acrobatics as well. I used to practice the splits, handstands, headstands, flips."

5. Mary Earps, born in 1993 in Nottingham, England, began playing football with her brother and father at age eight.

6. After earning her first senior cap for the Lionesses in 2017, she didn't become the starting goalkeeper until 2021.

7. In 2022, Earps helped the Lionesses secure their first-ever Women's Euro title, defeating Germany, 2–1.

8. Despite England losing to Spain, 1–0, in the 2023 Women's World Cup final, Earps won the Golden Glove for best goalkeeper.

9. Earps speaks often about the power of positive thinking: "The most important thing in the world is for you to be happy and do what you love. And if that's football—it's the greatest sport in the world—you should definitely do that."

10. Mary Earps was named the Best FIFA Women's Goalkeeper in both 2023 and 2024.

4 WINNERS OF THE WOMEN'S FIFA YOUNG PLAYER AWARD

The FIFA Young Player Award was introduced at the 2011 Women's World Cup in Germany. It recognizes one outstanding performance during each tournament. The award is selected by the FIFA Technical Study Group. Winners of the Women's FIFA Young Player Award must be 21 years old or younger.

Year	Winner	Nation	Age	Position
2023	Salma Paralluelo	Spain	19	Midfielder
2019	Giulia Gwinn	Germany	20	Midfielder
2015	Kadeisha Buchanan	Canada	19	Defender
2011	Caitlin Foord	Australia	16	Defender/midfielder

WHO MIGHT BE NEXT?
43 RISING WOMEN'S STARS FROM AROUND THE WORLD

Here are some football talents (born in 2003 or after) who could shine at the next Women's World Cups.

1. **Mara Alber** is a creative midfielder from Germany. She made her professional soccer debut at age 16.

2. **Korbin Albert**, a midfielder from Illinois, scored her first goal for the U.S. women's national team against Australia at the 2024 Olympics. She was the squad's second-youngest player, after Jaedyn Shaw.

3. **Amanda Allen** was born in Mississauga, Ontario, to parents from Jamaica. The forward earned her first cap for the Canadian national team in 2022.

4. Center back **Brooke Aspin** played for England's under-23 squad in 2023.

5. **Linda Caicedo**, a striker on the Colombian women's national team, scored two goals at the 2023 Women's World Cup. Her efforts helped Colombia secure victories over South Korea and, in a major upset, Germany.

6. **Milly Clegg** scored her first international goal as a striker for the New Zealand national team in 2024. At 17, she was the youngest player in New Zealand's squad for the 2023 Women's World Cup.

7. **Hapsatou Malado Diallo** became the first woman from Senegal to play professionally in Spain in 2023. She is a striker and considers Cristiano Ronaldo her inspiration.

8. Italian midfielder **Giulia Dragoni** represented her country at the 2023 Women's World Cup. At 16, she was the youngest player in the competition's history—this century. (Carolina Morace was 14 when she played for Italy in 1978.)

9. Dudinha, a Brazilian midfielder, launched her professional career in 2023 in São Paulo, Brazil. She played in Brazil's under-20 squad in 2024.

10. Melchie Dumornay, at 16, earned her first cap for the Haitian women's national team in 2020. She helped guide the team to its first Women's World Cup in 2023. By the end of 2024, she had already scored 16 goals for Haiti.

11. English striker **Mia Enderby** signed with Liverpool at age 18. The manager called her "direct, quick, and capable of scoring all types of goals."

12. Laurina Fazer, a midfielder from Argenteuil, France, played three games for her country in 2023. She launched her professional career at Paris Saint-Germain in 2020.

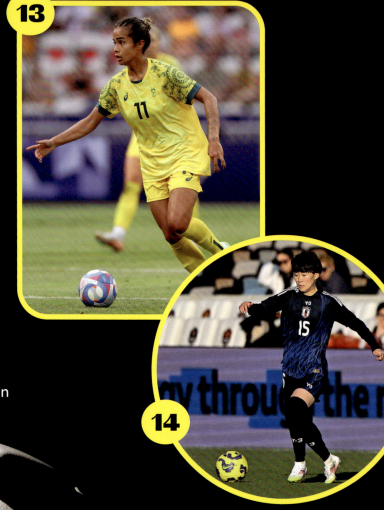

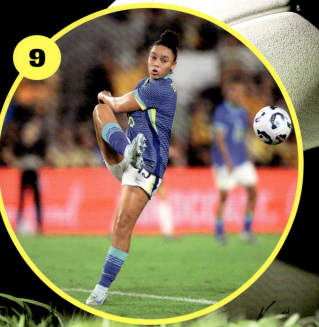

13. Mary Fowler, at 16, was Australia's youngest player at the 2019 Women's World Cup. She went on to score for her national team in the 2020 Olympics and the 2023 Women's World Cup.

14. Aoba Fujino, a forward from Tokyo, Japan, joined the senior national team in 2022. She scored against Costa Rica in the 2023 Women's World Cup and against Spain at the 2024 Olympics.

15. Daniela Galic is an Australian of Croatian descent. At age 16, she signed a pro contract for Melbourne City. The forward has played for the Australian women's national team since 2024.

16. Signe Gaupset is a midfielder from Molde, Norway. She debuted on the Norwegian women's national team in 2024, scoring against Albania in the Women's Euro 2025 qualifying playoffs.

17. Brazilian forward **Aline Gomes**, also known simply as Aline, scored her first NWSL goal in 2024 for North Carolina Courage at age 19. She has been on the Brazilian women's national team since 2023.

18. Ana María Guzmán is a defender from Colombia. Her first international appearance was at the 2023 Women's World Cup.

19. Maika Hamano, a forward born in Osaka, Japan, scored against Nigeria at the 2024 Olympics in France. She joined the Japanese women's national team in 2022 and was part of the 2023 Women's World Cup squad.

20. At 19, defensive midfielder **Claire Hutton** from Bethlehem, New York, debuted for the senior U.S. team—in the starting lineup at the 2025 SheBelieves Cup.

21. Liana Joseph is a French footballer of Haitian descent who plays as a forward. She competed on France's under-20 team in 2024.

22. Rosa Kafaji (22), a Swedish forward of Iraqi descent, began playing professionally in 2019. She has been a member of Sweden's women's national team since 2023.

23. At 17, **Wieke Kaptein**, a midfielder from the Netherlands, became the youngest Dutch player ever selected for a World Cup in 2023.

24. Goalkeeper **Khiara Keating** was called up to the England national team for the first time in 2023. She started her pro career at Manchester City.

25. Toko Koga, born in Osaka, Japan, is a defender but scored her first goal for Japan's senior national team in 2024.

26. Kathrine Kühl is a defensive midfielder for Denmark's national women's team. She was the youngest member of the Danish Women's World Cup squad in 2023.

27. Vicky López has played as a midfielder for the Spanish women's national team since 2024. For goal celebrations, she points to the sky in memory of her mother.

28. Clara Luvanga has played as a striker for Tanzania's women's national team since 2024.

29. Olivia Moultrie is an attacking midfielder from Wilsonville, Oregon. At 18, she scored a brace for the U.S. women's national team in a 5–0 rout of the Dominican Republic in 2024. Moultrie wears number 13, Alex Morgan's old number.

30. Forward **Sara Ortega** started her pro career at Athletic Club in Spain at age 16. She played for Spain's under-19 squad in 2023.

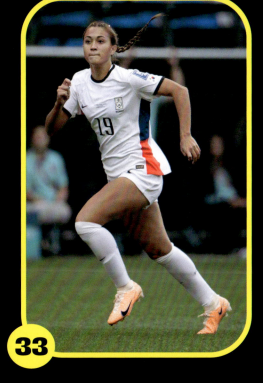

34. Sheika Scott represented the Costa Rica national team in 2022. The midfielder attended the 2023 Women's World Cup as part of the 23-player squad. Her hero is former team captain Shirley Cruz.

35. Ally Sentnor, a forward from Hanson, Massachusetts, earned two caps for the U.S. women's national team in 2024. She shares her hometown with U.S. soccer stars and sisters Kristie and Sam Mewis. That same year, Sentnor was named U.S. Soccer Young Female Player of the Year.

36. At 18, **Jaedyn Shaw** of Frisco, Texas, was selected as the 2022 U.S. Soccer Young Female Player of the Year. She now plays for the U.S. women's national team.

31. Forward **Salma Paralluelo** from Zaragoza, Spain, made her national team debut at age 19. Paralluelo is the first person to have won World Cups at three levels—the FIFA Women's World Cup in 2023 as well as the 2022 under-20 and 2018 under-17 tournaments.

32. Alex Pfeiffer, a forward from St. Louis, Missouri, notched her first professional goal in 2024 for the Kansas City Current at age 16. She plays for the United States at the youth international level.

33. Casey Yu-jin Phair, born in South Korea, was raised in New Jersey. The striker netted four goals for the South Korean national team in 2023 and 2024. She launched her pro career with Angel City FC in 2024.

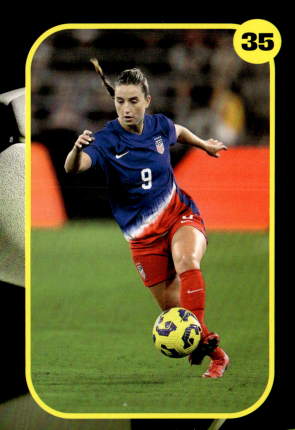

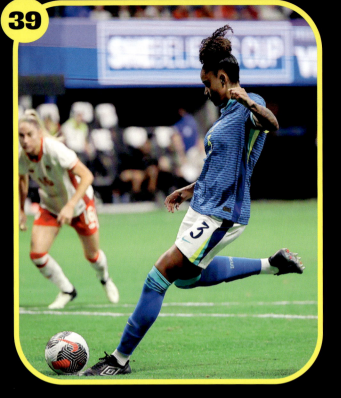

39. Tarciane was called up to Brazil's national team in 2022 by then head coach Pia Sundhage. At the 2024 SheBelieves Cup, the center back scored her first goal for Brazil with a penalty kick against Canada.

40. U.S. forward **Alyssa Thompson** scored in her regular-season professional debut for Angel City FC in 2023 at age 18.

41. Gisele Thompson is a right back from Studio City, California. She earned her first senior U.S. national team cap in 2025. Her older sister, Alyssa, plays as a forward on the national team.

37. Alice Soto, an attacking midfielder from Salamanca, became the youngest player, at 12, to register with the Mexican Football Federation, in 2018. She scored her first professional goal at 14 and scored a brace in her senior debut, a friendly against Thailand in 2024.

38. Momoko Tanikawa, a midfielder from Aichi, Japan, scored the winning goal against Brazil in the group stage at the 2024 Olympics. The U.S. later defeated Japan in the quarterfinals, with Trinity Rodman scoring in extra time.

42. McKenna "Mak" Whitham from Granite Bay, California, became the youngest female to play in a regular-season U.S. pro soccer match in 2025. She debuted for NY Gotham FC at age 14.

43. Lily Yohannes, born to Eritrean parents in Springfield, Virginia, moved to the Netherlands at age 10. After playing for Dutch youth teams, she chose to represent the United States and, at 16, became the youngest player at senior camp since Sophia Smith (now Wilson) in 2017. While at Ajax, the midfielder scored her first international goal for the U.S. in 2024.

SHOW ME THE MONEY

42 FACTS ABOUT WORLD CUP COIN

1. Hosting a World Cup is expensive.

2. FIFA does not pay nations or cities for hosting the tournament.

3. The host nation Qatar spent an estimated $220 billion in preparation for the 2022 World Cup.

4. Qatar built transportation, hotels, and stadiums to host the 2022 tournament.

5. The 2022 tournament was the most expensive—and criticized—World Cup in history.

6. Hosting a World Cup can bring income to a country and its soccer federation.

7. The 2022 World Cup in Qatar generated over $685 million in ticket sales.

8. Fees paid for luxury seating and special access at the 2022 World Cup totaled nearly $243 million.

9. The 2026 World Cup was projected to earn the U.S., Mexico, and Canada as much as $5 billion.

10. FIFA has registered the term "World Cup" as a U.S. trademark.

11. Out of all the World Cup hosts, the United States in 1994 made the most money on its investment.

12. More than 3.5 million soccer fans in total attended the 1994 World Cup.

13. The 1994 tournament finished with a profit of about $50 million. That's more than twice what was expected.

14. The United States used its profits from hosting the 1994 World Cup to create the U.S. Soccer Foundation.

15. Each national team that qualified for the 2022 World Cup received $1.5 million.

16. Each national team that reached the group stage of the 2023 Women's World Cup earned $1.56 million.

17. For the first time, each of the 732 players were paid $30,000 for qualifying for the 2023 Women's World Cup.

18. Each player on the Spanish national team was awarded $270,000 for winning the Women's World Cup in 2023.

19. The total prize money for the 2022 World Cup was $440 million—four times more than the 2023 Women's World Cup.

20. According to FIFA, one reason for the smaller prize pool for the Women's World Cup is that it receives between "10 and 100 times" less from sponsors and broadcasters.

21. In 2019, the U.S. women's national team home jersey became the best-selling item in a single season on Nike.com.

22. Some corporate brands have committed to spending equal dollars on women's and men's sports sponsorships.

23. FIFA has said it intends to make the prize money equal between men's and women's games by 2027.

24. When U.S. Soccer hired Emma Hayes of England in 2024, she became the highest-paid women's soccer coach in the world.

25. Mauricio Pochettino of Argentina became the highest-paid coach in the history of the U.S. men's national team in 2024. His salary was reportedly $6 million.

26. Diego Simeone, coach of La Liga club Atlético de Madrid, was paid $33.5 million in 2025. That's more than any other soccer manager, even Manchester City's Pep Guardiola.

27. FIFA makes the most money for World Cup tournaments from selling the rights to show games on TV and streaming platforms.

31. Netflix signed a broadcast deal with FIFA for the 2027 and 2031 Women's World Cups for an unknown sum.

32. Out of the 10 professional sports leagues with the highest broadcast revenue, four are soccer leagues.

33. The top soccer leagues for broadcast revenue are the English Premier League, La Liga (Spain), Bundesliga (Germany), and Serie A (Italy).

34. FIFA pays soccer clubs to let their players compete for their national teams in the World Cup.

35. FIFA paid 440 soccer clubs over $200 million for player release to the 2022 World Cup.

36. For the 2026 and 2030 World Cups, the FIFA payment to clubs for releasing players increased to $355 million.

37. The broadcasting deal for the 2025 FIFA Club World Cup is estimated at $1 billion. This international club tournament, now held every four years, features 32 club teams from all the federations.

38. FIFA has announced $1 billion in prize money for the FIFA 2025 Club World Cup.

39. But money isn't everything.

40. Some of the highest-paid players—Belgium's Kevin De Bruyne and Spain's Rodri—have complained about the growing number of scheduled club and international matches.

41. Soccer players argue the packed football calendar is leading to mental and physical burnout.

42. "It's difficult to be sharp if you play over 70 games a year," said Norwegian striker Erling Haaland.

28. A record 1.5 billion people worldwide watched Argentina defeat the defending champion France in Qatar's 2022 World Cup final.

29. The most watched NFL Super Bowl, by comparison, was the 2025 championship, with almost 128 million viewers.

30. FIFA made almost $2.9 billion from broadcasting rights in 2022.

GAME CHANGER
Landon Donovan

1. Born in 1982, Landon Donovan grew up in Redlands, California.

2. A talented high school player, he joined the U.S. national under-17 team in 1998.

3. At just 20, Donovan helped the U.S. national team reach the 2002 World Cup quarterfinals.

4. At the 2010 World Cup, Landon Donovan won the FIFA Young Player Award. He is the only American to have earned that honor.

5. Donovan won a record six MLS Cups with the San Jose Earthquakes and the L.A. Galaxy between 2001 and 2014.

6. Donovan also holds the all-time Major League Soccer record for assists, with 136.

7. A statue was unveiled outside the L.A. Galaxy stadium in 2021 to honor Donovan's impact on the U.S. pro league.

8. In his international and pro career, Donovan converted 51 of 56 penalties.

9. Donovan notched five goals in three World Cups, making him the highest-scoring U.S. men's player in the history of the World Cup.

10. At the 2010 World Cup, Donovan scored a thrilling goal in stoppage time against Algeria. "It was a transformative moment for how the game was received in the United States," football commentator Ian Darke later explained. "That kind of explosive moment at the end made a lot of people realize what incredible drama soccer can offer."

WORLD CUP MONEY:
16 PRIZE POOLS

How much does the World Cup winner earn? Argentina—the 2022 men's World Cup champions—won $42 million. The Spanish women's national team won $4.29 million for taking the 2023 Women's World Cup title.

5 WOMEN'S WORLD CUP PRIZE POOLS

World Cup	Total Prize Money*	Winner
Australia and New Zealand 2023	$110 million	$4.29 million
France 2019	$30 million	$4 million
Canada 2015	$15 million	$2 million
Germany 2011	$10 million	$1 million
China 2007	$5.8 million	$1 million

Source: FIFA, FIFPRO

* = The Women's World Cup didn't have prize money until 2007

11 MEN'S WORLD CUP PRIZE POOLS

World Cup	Total Prize Money*	Winner
Qatar 2022	$440 million	$42 million
Russia 2018	$400 million	$38 million
Brazil 2014	$358 million	$35 million
South Africa 2010	$348 million	$30 million
Germany 2006	$236 million	$20 million
Japan and South Korea 2002	$134 million	$8 million
France 1998	NA	$6 million
USA 1994	NA	$4 million
Italy 1990	NA	$3.5 million
Mexico 1986	NA	$2.8 million
Spain 1982	NA	$2.2 million

Source: *The Athletic*

* = Data was only available starting in 2002.

50 MAJOR MLS FACTS

1. Creating a professional soccer league was part of the U.S.'s bid to host the 1994 World Cup.

2. Major League Soccer launched two years after the United States hosted the 1994 World Cup.

3. DC United won the first MLS Cup in 1996. They defeated the Los Angeles Galaxy in extra time, 3–2, on a rain-soaked pitch in Foxborough, Massachusetts.

4. The goal of Major League Soccer (MLS) was to tap into a growing popularity of soccer in the United States.

5. There are now 30 teams in Major League Soccer, 27 from the United States and three from Canada.

6. The three Canadian teams are Toronto FC, Vancouver Whitecaps FC, and CF Montreal.

7. Canadian defender Alphonso Davies began his pro career at the Vancouver Whitecaps in 2015 before transferring to Bayern Munich.

8. Alphonso Davies scored Canada's first-ever men's World Cup goal in 2022, against Croatia in the group stage.

9. San Diego FC is the newest Major League Soccer club.

10. Major League Soccer has added a new team each season since 2005.

11. Major League Soccer is the second-most attended league in the world, after the English Premier League.

12. More than 12 million fans attended MLS games in 2024.

13. In 2024, two MLS matches drew crowds that surpassed 70,000.

14. Lionel Messi of Inter Miami won the 2024 MLS MVP, with 20 goals in 19 appearances.

15. Inter Miami signed Lionel Messi to a contract worth $150 million in 2023.

16. The year following Messi's signing to Inter Miami, the MLS club saw their revenue double.

17. Inter Miami paid the most for player salaries of any MLS team—a total of $41.7 million—in 2024.

18. CF Montreal spent only about $11.5 million on player salaries, the least of any MLS club, in 2024.

19. Major League Soccer features players born in 79 different nations.

20. The MLS is more diverse than any other North American sports league.

21. The NBA ranks second, with players from 45 countries.

22. The MLS has players from more countries than the English Premier League, France's Ligue 1, Italy's Serie A, Spain's La Liga, or Germany's Bundesliga.

23. What country produced the most MLS players born outside of North America in 2024? Argentina, with 35, including Messi.

24. Brazil (30) and Colombia (29) ranked second and third for nations with most MLS players.

25. The MLS Designated Player rule, introduced in 2007, allows teams to sign international stars outside of their salary caps.

26. A salary cap limits how much a professional sports team can spend on player salaries.

27. What's the point of a salary cap? It prevents the wealthiest teams from signing all the top players.

28. A salary cap also helps a sports league stay financially sound and competitive.

29. The MLS Designated Player rule is sometimes called the Beckham rule.

30. In 2007, the L.A. Galaxy signed David Beckham to a $32.5 million contract over five years.

31. David Beckham scored 18 goals and had 40 assists in 98 games over five seasons with the L.A. Galaxy.

32. A David Beckham statue has stood outside the L.A. Galaxy stadium since 2019.

33. Thierry Henry of France, Zlatan Ibrahimovic of Sweden, and Wayne Rooney of England have also played in the MLS as Designated Players.

34. Wayne Rooney left Everton as DC United's Designated Player in 2018.

35. After retiring as a player, Rooney was named head coach of DC United for a year.

36. MLS teams may sign up to three players who are 22 and younger (U-22), which don't count against their salary caps.

37. Federico Redondo of Argentina and Dejan Joveljic from Serbia joined the MLS as U-22 players in 2024.

38. Diego Luna, who debuted for the U.S. national team in 2024, also joined the MLS as a U-22 player.

39. Almost half of MLS players are from the United States and Canada.

40. California has produced more MLS players than any other U.S. state.

41. Chris Wondolowski of Danville, California, scored 171 goals in the MLS. He retired in 2021. His record still stands.

42. A member of the Kiowa tribe, Wondolowski became the first person of American Indian heritage to play in the World Cup, in 2014.

43. Major League Soccer has developed plenty of young U.S. talent since it launched.

44. Tyler Adams, Weston McKennie, and Ricardo Pepi began their careers in the MLS before moving to top European clubs.

45. The MLS team with the best regular-season record wins the Supporters' Shield.

46. The annual MLS Cup final pits the Eastern Conference champions against the Western Conference champions.

47. The winner of the MLS Cup earns a place in North America's top club competition, Concacaf Champions Cup.

48. The Los Angeles Galaxy won the 2024 MLS Cup, defeating the NY Red Bulls, 2–1.

49. The winners of the Concacaf Champions Cup qualify for the FIFA Club World Cup, which takes place every four years.

50. The Concacaf Champions Cup winners also earn a spot in the FIFA Intercontinental Cup, an annual tournament that kicked off in 2024.

THE MLS CUP:
29 CHAMPIONS AND THEIR CHALLENGERS

Major League Soccer (MLS) started in 1996 with 10 teams. The L.A. Galaxy holds the record for most MLS Cup victories, with six titles. Here are the 29 champions, challengers, and most valuable players (MVP) from the finals.

Year	Champion	Challenger	Score	MVP (Final)
2024	Los Angeles Galaxy	NY Red Bulls	2–1	Gastón Brugman
2023	Columbus Crew	Los Angeles FC	2–1	Cucho Hernández
2022	Los Angeles FC	Philadelphia Union	3–3 (3–0)*	John McCarthy
2021	New York City FC	Portland Timbers	1–1 (4–2)*	Sean Johnson
2020	Columbus Crew	Seattle Sounders FC	3–0	Lucas Zelarayán
2019	Seattle Sounders FC	Toronto FC	3–1	Víctor Rodríguez
2018	Atlanta United	Portland Timbers	2–0	Josef Martínez
2017	Toronto FC	Seattle Sounders FC	2–0	Jozy Altidore
2016	Seattle Sounders FC	Toronto FC	0–0 (5–4)*	Stefan Frei
2015	Portland Timbers	Columbus Crew	2–1	Diego Valeri
2014	Los Angeles Galaxy	New England Revolution	2–1**	Robbie Keane
2013	Sporting Kansas City	Real Salt Lake	1–1 (7–6)*	Aurélien Collin
2012	Los Angeles Galaxy	Houston Dynamo FC	3–1	Omar Gonzalez
2011	Los Angeles Galaxy	Houston Dynamo FC	1–0	Landon Donovan
2010	Colorado Rapids	FC Dallas	2–1**	Conor Casey
2009	Real Salt Lake	Los Angeles Galaxy	1–1 (5–4)*	Nick Rimando
2008	Columbus Crew	NY Red Bulls	3–1	Guillermo Barros Schelotto
2007	Houston Dynamo FC	New England Revolution	2–1	Dwayne De Rosario
2006	Houston Dynamo FC	New England Revolution	1–1 (4–3)*	Brian Ching
2005	Los Angeles Galaxy	New England Revolution	1–0**	Guillermo Ramírez
2004	DC United	Kansas City Wizards	3–2	Alecko Eskandarian
2003	San Jose Earthquakes	Chicago Fire FC	4–2	Landon Donovan
2002	Los Angeles Galaxy	New England Revolution	1–0**	Carlos Ruiz
2001	San Jose Earthquakes	Los Angeles Galaxy	2–1**	Dwayne De Rosario
2000	Kansas City Wizards	Chicago Fire FC	1–0	Tony Meola
1999	DC United	Los Angeles Galaxy	2–0	Ben Olsen
1998	Chicago Fire FC	DC United	2–0	Peter Nowak
1997	DC United	Colorado Rapids	2–1	Jaime Moreno
1996	DC United	Los Angeles Galaxy	3–2**	Marco Etcheverry

* = Match decided in penalty kicks (shootout score in parentheses).
** = Match decided in extra time.

52 FACTS ABOUT THE NWSL

1. The first professional U.S. soccer league for women was the Women's United Soccer Association (WUSA).

2. Mia Hamm, Julie Foudy, and Kristine Lilly, along with their 1999 Women's World Cup champion teammates, signed on to play in the WUSA.

3. The WUSA launched with fanfare in 2001.

4. The WUSA folded without fanfare, five days before the opening of the 2003 Women's World Cup in the United States.

5. Next came Women's Professional Soccer, the WPS, in 2009. (Marta played for Los Angeles Sol.)

6. The WPS lasted only three years.

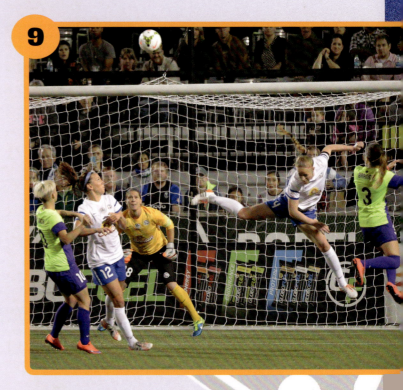

7. The National Women's Soccer League (NWSL) kicked off with eight clubs in 2013.

8. The first NWSL MVP was Lauren Holiday, with 12 goals and nine assists over 18 matches.

9. Holiday (12) was the first NWSL player to have her jersey retired.

10. Four of the original eight NWSL clubs are still active—Chicago Red Stars, Portland Thorns FC, Seattle Reign FC, and Washington Spirit (in Washington, DC).

11. One club has changed its name: Sky Blue FC is now NY Gotham FC.

12. Another club changed its name and moved: Western New York Flash became North Carolina Courage.

13. The league added Houston Dash in 2014 and Orlando Pride in 2016.

14. In 2015, Crystal Dunn of the Washington Spirit won the NWSL Golden Boot, with 15 goals in 20 games.

15. In 2024, Temwa Chawinga of Kansas City Current broke the NWSL record for most goals in a single season—20 goals in 25 games.

16. The Boston Breakers and FC Kansas City both folded in 2017 (the same year Rose Lavelle began her NWSL career).

17. Today's NWSL has 14 clubs, with one in Boston, Massachusetts, and another in Denver, Colorado, set to join in 2026.

18. The newest NWSL teams are Bay FC, Utah Royals FC, San Diego Wave FC, Angel City FC, Racing Louisville FC, and Kansas City Current.

19. The KC Current play in CPKC Stadium in Kansas City, Missouri, the world's first soccer stadium built for a professional women's team.

20. CPKC Stadium seats 11,500 fans, none of whom are more than 100 feet (30 meters) from the touchline.

21. More than two million fans attended NWSL games in 2024.

22. Americans Lindsey Horan (now Heaps), Lynn Williams (now Biyendolo), and Sophia Smith (now Wilson) have earned NWSL MVP titles.

23. League MVP winners have also included many international players.

24. Temwa Chawinga (who is from Malawi), Kerolin (Brazil), and Sam Kerr (Australia) have won NWSL MVP titles.

25. Jenna Nighswonger was NWSL Rookie of the Year in 2023, followed by Croix Bethune in 2024.

26. Rose Lavelle (2017), Emily Sonnett (2016), and Crystal Dunn (2014) were all number-one overall NWSL draft picks. They've lived up to the hype.

27. Since 2020, Sophia Smith (now Wilson), Emily Fox, and Naomi Girma were all number-one overall NWSL draft picks. They've also lived up to the hype.

28. Angel City FC selected Alyssa Thompson as the number-one overall pick in the 2023 NWSL draft.

29. The Utah Royals chose Ally Sentnor for the top draft selection in 2024.

30. A 15-year-old attacking midfielder, Olivia Moultrie, joined the Portland Thorns in 2021 and won the NWSL Championship the following year.

31. It was Olivia Moultrie who successfully challenged the NWSL rule against players under 18.

32. Jaedyn Shaw of San Diego Wave scored in each of her first three professional games in 2022 at age 17.

33. The NWSL record for the fastest goal—only 22 seconds into the match—was set by Michelle Cooper of Kansas City Current in her rookie year.

34. The NWSL has a 26-match regular season schedule.

35. The NWSL Shield is awarded to the team that finishes in first place at the end of the regular season.

36. The Challenge Cup pits the previous season's NWSL Shield winner against the reigning NWSL champion.

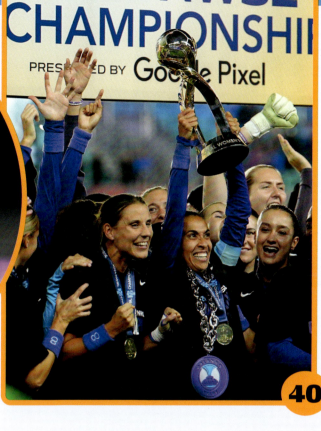

37. The Challenge Cup is held at the beginning of each season.

38. The top eight NWSL teams qualify for the playoffs.

39. The postseason begins with four quarterfinal matches, followed by the semifinals and the NWSL Championship Final, typically in November.

40. The Orlando Pride won the 2024 NWSL Championship, defeating the Washington Spirit, 1–0.

41. The NWSL agreed to eliminate its draft in 2024.

42. All NWSL players now have free agency.

43. Free agency means a pro athlete can negotiate a contract with any team.

44. In 2013, the first season of the NWSL, the minimum salary for players was $6,000.

45. In a 2023 survey of Women's World Cup players, one in three earned less than $30,000 a year from soccer.

46. One in five Women's World Cup players in 2023 had a second job to support themselves.

47. Alyssa Thompson, along with her sister, Gisele, became the first high school athletes to sign a NIL deal with Nike in 2022.

48. *NIL* stands for name, image, and likeness.

49. McKenna "Mak" Whitham, at 13, became the youngest athlete in any sport to sign a NIL deal with Nike in 2024.

50. The NWSL struck a $240-million, four-year media rights deal in 2024.

51. $240 million is 40 times the value of the NWSL's previous broadcast contract.

52. Notable investors in NWSL clubs include sports figures Patrick Mahomes, Kevin Durant, and Serena Williams, and actors Natalie Portman, Jennifer Garner, and America Ferrera.

WOMEN'S U.S. PRO SOCCER:
18 CHAMPIONS AND THEIR CHALLENGERS

The Women's United Soccer Association (2001–2003) and the Women's Professional Soccer league (2009–2012) didn't last very long. But the National Women's Soccer League (NWSL) has been going strong since 2013. Here are the 18 champions, challengers, and most valuable players (MVP) from each league's finals.

Year	Champion	Challenger	Score	MVP (Final)
2024	Orlando Pride	Washington Spirit	1–0	Barbra Banda
2023	NJ/NY Gotham FC	OL Reign	2–1	Midge Purce
2022	Portland Thorns FC	Kansas City Current	2–0	Sophia Smith (now Wilson)
2021	Washington Spirit	Chicago Red Stars	2–1**	Aubrey Bledsoe (now Kingsbury)
2020	No championship final held			
2019	North Carolina Courage	Chicago Red Stars	4–0	Debinha
2018	North Carolina Courage	Portland Thorns FC	3–0	Jessica McDonald
2017	Portland Thorns FC	North Carolina Courage	1–0	Lindsey Horan (now Heaps)
2016	Western New York Flash	Washington Spirit	2–2 (3–2)*	Sabrina D'Angelo
2015	FC Kansas City	Seattle Reign FC	1–0	Amy Rodriguez
2014	FC Kansas City	Seattle Reign FC	2–1	Lauren Holiday
2013	Portland Thorns FC	Western New York Flash	2–0	Tobin Heath
2011	Western New York Flash	Philadelphia Independence	1–1 (5–4)*	Christine Sinclair
2010	FC Gold Pride	Philadelphia Independence	4–0	Marta
2009	Sky Blue FC	Los Angeles Sol	1–0	Heather O'Reilly
2003	Washington Freedom	Atlanta Beat	2–1**	Abby Wambach
2002	Carolina Courage	Washington Freedom	3–2	Birgit Prinz
2001	Bay Area CyberRays	Atlanta Beat	3–3 (4–2)*	Julie Murray

* = Match decided in penalty kicks (shootout score in parentheses).

** = Match decided in extra time.

GAME CHANGER

Trinity Rodman

1. Born in 2002 in Laguna Niguel, California, Trinity Rodman started playing soccer at age four.

2. Rodman, the daughter of NBA legend Dennis Rodman, and her older brother were raised by her single mother.

3. By age 10, Trinity was playing for So Cal Blues, a top girls' soccer club.

4. Originally set to play soccer at Washington State University, she chose the NWSL instead due to the pandemic.

5. When Rodman was drafted in the first round by the Washington Spirit, the 18-year-old had never even been to Washington, DC.

6. She scored just minutes after entering her first professional soccer match in 2021.

7. In her debut season, Rodman won the 2021 NWSL Championship, was named NWSL Rookie of the Year, and earned a spot on the NWSL Best XI.

8. The forward made her senior U.S. women's national team debut in 2022, the year after she was named the U.S. Soccer Young Female Player of the Year.

9. At the 2024 Olympics, she scored three goals and helped the U.S. women's team win a gold medal.

10. Rodman loves to play *Fortnite*: "I pack my entire PlayStation, all the cords, two controllers, just in case people want to play with me. It's my stress reliever."

10 HIGHEST-PAID MEN'S SOCCER PLAYERS

Soccer players are among the highest-paid athletes in the world, and Cristiano Ronaldo is at the top. His earnings from playing soccer (on-field) plus money from endorsements, licensing, appearances, and businesses (off-field) totaled $285 million in 2024.

Player	Country	On-field*	Off-field
Cristiano Ronaldo	Portugal	$220 million	$65 million
Karim Benzema	France	$100 million	$4 million
Neymar	Brazil	$80 million	$30 million
Kylian Mbappé	France	$70 million	$4 million
Lionel Messi	Argentina	$60 million	$75 million
Sadio Mané	Senegal	$48 million	$4 million
Erling Haaland	Norway	$46 million	$14 million
Vinícius Júnior	Brazil	$40 million	$15 million
Kevin De Bruyne	Belgium	$35 million	$4 million
Mohamed Salah	Egypt	$35 million	$18 million

Source: *Forbes*, 2024

* = Total includes annual base salaries, bonuses, and some club-based image-rights agreements.

GAME CHANGER
Cristiano Ronaldo

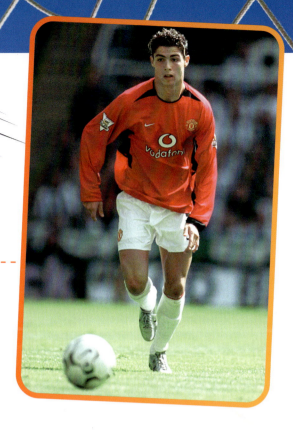

1. Cristiano Ronaldo was born in 1985 in Funchal, Madeira, Portugal into a working-class family. His exceptional soccer talent was clear from an early age.

2. At 18, in 2003, he made his senior debut for both Portugal and Manchester United.

3. At the 2022 World Cup, Ronaldo became the first men's player to score in five different World Cups.

4. Throughout his career, he has also played for Real Madrid, Juventus, and Al-Nassr FC.

5. He holds the record as Real Madrid's all-time top scorer with 450 goals.

6. Ronaldo is also the all-time top scorer in the UEFA Champions League with 140 goals.

7. He has won the Ballon d'Or five times (2008, 2013, 2014, 2016, and 2017).

8. Ronaldo was also named FIFA Player of the Year in 2008, 2016, and 2017.

9. On September 5, 2024, Ronaldo scored his 900th official career goal with a volley in the 34th minute during Portugal's UEFA Nations League match against Croatia. He was the first soccer player to reach this milestone.

10. "It was emotional because it's a milestone," Ronaldo said. "Only I know, and the people around me, how hard it is to work every day, to be physically and psychologically fit, to score 900 goals. It's a unique milestone in my career."

11 HIGHEST-PAID WOMEN'S SOCCER PLAYERS

The top players in the NWSL, the Women's Super League (WSL) in England, Spain's Liga F, and France's Première Ligue earn annual salaries of more than $500,000. That number doesn't include off-field earnings. In 2024, *Forbes* reported Alex Morgan earned $7 million in endorsements.

Player	Country	On-field*
Aitana Bonmatí	Spain	More than $1 million
Alexia Putellas	Spain	$728,000
Sam Kerr	Australia	$560,000
Sophia Wilson	U.S.	More than $500,000
María Sánchez	U.S.	About $500,000
Keira Walsh	England	$476,000
Ada Hegerberg	Norway	$400,000
Crystal Dunn	U.S.	$400,000
Marta	Brazil	$400,000
Mallory Swanson	U.S.	$400,000
Nadine Angerer	Germany	$400,000

Source: *Essentially Sports*, 2024

* = Salaries in women's football are not public, so these figures are estimates.

GAME CHANGER

Naomi Girma

1. U.S. coach Emma Hayes said of Naomi Girma: "[She] is the best defender I've ever seen. Ever. She's got everything: poise, composure, she defends, she anticipates, she leads."

2. Born in 2000 in San Jose, California, Girma is the first Ethiopian American to play for the U.S. national women's team.

3. Until age 10, she played for a soccer club organized by her father.

4. "My dad loved soccer and that started with his childhood in Ethiopia," Girma said. "Just being in the Ethiopian culture and seeing how much appreciation there was for soccer was amazing, and I think that really helped me fall in love with it."

5. After joining a youth soccer club, she was soon invited to an under-14 U.S. national team camp.

6. Girma played at Stanford University after high school, leading the team to the 2019 NCAA championship title as captain.

7. In 2022, Girma was named NWSL Rookie of the Year after being drafted by San Diego Wave.

8. The following year, she was named the U.S. Soccer Female Player of the Year.

9. At the 2024 Olympics, the center back led the U.S. to a gold medal, playing every minute of the competition.

10. Naomi Girma set a world record for women's soccer in 2025: she signed with the English club Chelsea for a $1.1 million transfer fee.

BEYOND THE CUP

75 FACTS ABOUT OLYMPIC SOCCER

1. Soccer was one of the first Olympic team sports.

2. In addition to soccer, they played cricket, water polo, and tug of war.

3. The U.S. entered a team in the tug of war event in 1908. They didn't medal.

4. In the soccer competition at the 1900 Olympics in Paris, nations were represented by club teams.

5. But soccer wasn't formally recognized as an Olympic event until 1908.

6. At the 1912 Olympics in Stockholm, Sweden, Great Britain defeated Denmark, 4–2, to win the gold medal in men's soccer.

7. Great Britain—England, Scotland, and Wales—and Northern Ireland compete as one Olympic team, now called Team GB.

8. Women's soccer didn't appear at the Olympics until 1996.

9. The United States claimed the first Olympic gold medal in women's soccer.

10. The U.S. women's team beat China, 2–1, in the first Olympic final in Atlanta, Georgia.

11. The Olympics were not held in 1916 (because of World War I).

12. They also were not held in 1940 and 1944 (because of World War II).

13. FIFA withdrew soccer as an event from the 1932 Olympics in Los Angeles.

14. FIFA's goal was to promote the second World Cup, which was to take place in 1934.

15. Sophus Nielsen of Denmark and Antal Dunai of Hungary share the record for most Olympic goals in the men's game—a lucky 13.

16. Nielsen played in the 1908 and 1912 Olympics, while Dunai played in 1968 and 1972.

17. Cristiane of Brazil holds the record for most all-time Olympic soccer goals. She scored five goals in 2004, five in 2008, two in 2012, and two in 2016.

18. In the past, professional athletes were not permitted to participate in the Olympics.

19. The Olympics allowed only amateur players.

20. An amateur athlete participates for fun, not as a career.

21. The amateur-only rules for the Olympics started to change in the 1970s.

22. Who could enjoy watching soccer without Pelé?

23. The 1984 Olympics included some professional soccer players for the first time.

24. Olympic basketball included its first U.S. pros, Michael Jordan and the Dream Team, in 1992.

25. The soccer event at the Olympics spans fewer days than the World Cup tournament.

26. Like the World Cup, Olympic soccer is divided into a group stage and a knockout stage.

27. Olympic soccer typically features fewer teams than the World Cup (16 men's and 12 women's teams played in 2024).

28. An Olympic soccer team has only 18 players, smaller than a World Cup squad.

29. Most of the male footballers at the Olympics must be 23 years old or younger (U-23).

30. But each country may select up to three older male players of the 18 total.

31. According to FIFA rules, men's professional soccer clubs are not required to release their players for the Olympics.

84 OLYMPIC MEDALS: MEN'S SOCCER

Men's soccer appeared at the Olympics for the first time in 1900. There were only three club teams and two matches that year.

Year	Gold	Silver	Bronze
Paris 2024	Spain	France	Morocco
Tokyo 2020	Brazil	Spain	Mexico
Rio 2016	Brazil	Germany	Nigeria
London 2012	Mexico	Brazil	South Korea
Beijing 2008	Argentina	Nigeria	Brazil
Athens 2004	Argentina	Paraguay	Italy
Sydney 2000	Cameroon	Spain	Chile
Atlanta 1996	Nigeria	Argentina	Brazil
Barcelona 1992	Spain	Poland	Ghana
Seoul 1988	Soviet Union	Brazil	West Germany
Los Angeles 1984	France	Brazil	Yugoslavia
Moscow 1980	Czechoslovakia	East Germany	Soviet Union
Montreal 1976	East Germany	Poland	Soviet Union
Munich 1972	Poland	Hungary	Soviet Union/East Germany
Mexico City 1968	Hungary	Bulgaria	Japan
Tokyo 1964	Hungary	Czechoslovakia	Germany
Rome 1960	Yugoslavia	Denmark	Hungary
Melbourne 1956	Soviet Union	Yugoslavia	Bulgaria
Helsinki 1952	Hungary	Yugoslavia	Sweden
London 1948	Sweden	Yugoslavia	Denmark
Berlin 1936	Italy	Austria	Norway
Amsterdam 1928	Uruguay	Argentina	Italy
Paris 1924	Uruguay	Switzerland	Sweden
Antwerp 1920	Belgium	Spain	Netherlands
Stockholm 1912	Great Britain	Denmark	Netherlands
London 1908**	Great Britain	Denmark	Netherlands
St. Louis 1904	Canada	Christian Brothers College*	St. Rose Parish*
Paris 1900	Great Britain	France	Belgium

* = U.S. school team

** = Medals were awarded for the first time; participants were national, not club or school, teams.

32. That's one reason Kylian Mbappé, Lionel Messi, and Christian Pulisic didn't participate in the 2024 Olympics.

33. That's also why U-23 Spanish stars Lamine Yamal and Nico Williams didn't play in the 2024 Olympics.

34. FIFA rules that limit elite players at the Olympics is a way of supporting the World Cup as soccer's top event.

35. Messi played in one Olympics—in 2008, at age 21.

36. Messi scored twice, leading Argentina to its second-ever gold medal.

37. At 20, Neymar won silver with Brazil at the 2012 Olympics.

38. Neymar said of the 2–1 gold-medal match loss to Mexico at a packed Wembley Stadium in London: "It was my first Games and I was so impressed with the whole thing. I'll remember it for the rest of my life."

39. Neymar captained Brazil—the Olympic host nation—to its first Olympic gold medal in 2016.

40. Neymar netted the decisive penalty in the final against Germany in 2016.

41. Brazil won its second gold medal at the 2020 Olympics in Tokyo, Japan.

42. Brazilian striker Richarlison scored a hat trick in his Olympic debut against Germany.

43. Two more goals made Richarlison the 2020 top Olympic scorer.

44. The youngest player on the 2000 U.S. men's Olympic soccer team was 18-year-old Landon Donovan.

45. Donovan came off the bench to score against Kuwait in his team's third match at the 2000 Olympics.

46. The late counterattack goal was so thrilling, the TV announcer—known for hollering "Goooooal!"—shouted it for 24 seconds, with a pause to breathe.

47. The U.S. men's soccer team earned a fourth-place finish in 2000.

48. More than 2,400 goals have been netted so far in the history of the men's Olympic football tournament.

49. In 2024, Spain won its second gold medal in men's soccer by beating host nation France, 5–3, in extra time.

50. Fermín López (11) and Sergio Camello of Spain each scored two goals in the 2024 Olympic football final.

51. Thierry Henry coached the French men to their first Olympic silver medal in 2024. (Their first gold medal in soccer was in 1984.)

52. Henry once held France's record for most men's international goals (51). Olivier Giroud broke it in 2022, retiring from the French team two years later with 57 goals.

53. Giroud won the 2018 World Cup but never played at the Olympics.

54. Only two men have won both Olympic gold and a World Cup since World War II—Argentines Ángel Di María and Lionel Messi.

55. African nations have won two Olympic gold medals for men's soccer: Nigeria in 1996 and Cameroon in 2000.

56. Great Britain and Hungary hold the record for the most Olympic gold medals in men's soccer—three.

57. Christine Pearce, formerly Rampone, helped lead the American women to three straight Olympic gold medals, in 2004, 2008, and 2012.

58. More than 40 women, including Americans Pearce and Mia Hamm, Anja Mittag of Germany, and Hege Riise of Norway, have won both an Olympic gold medal and a World Cup.

59. Formiga of Brazil played at every Olympics from 1996 to 2020.

60. Formiga holds the record for most appearances in women's soccer at the Olympics—seven.

61. Brazil, led by Marta, Formiga, and Cristiane, won Olympic silver in 2004 and 2008.

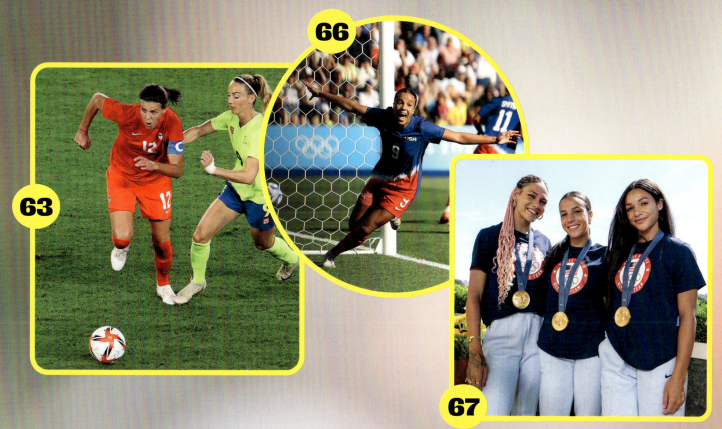

62. Onome Ebi of Nigeria, Homare Sawa of Japan, Christine Sinclair of Canada, and Brazil's Marta have all competed in six Olympic Games.

63. Christine Sinclair led Canada to three Olympic medals, including its first gold at the 2020 Olympics in Tokyo.

64. Former Swedish player Pia Sundhage coached the U.S. women's national team to two Olympic gold medals, in 2008 and 2012.

65. The United States triumphed over Brazil, 1–0, to take the gold medal in women's soccer at the 2024 Olympics.

66. Mallory Swanson scored her fourth tournament goal in the 2024 Olympic final.

67. Trinity Rodman, Mallory Swanson, and Sophia Wilson (then Smith) combined for 10 of 12 U.S. Olympic goals in 2024.

68. Some called the trio the Triple Espresso.

69. Wilson explained the nickname, first suggested by Rodman's half sister: "I feel like we're all a lot of energy. We're all feisty on the field, but we can be sweet."

70. Goalkeeper Alyssa Naeher and a defense led by Naomi Girma allowed only two goals at the 2024 Olympics.

71. The Olympics take place two years after the men's World Cup and the year after the Women's World Cup.

72. No team has ever won the Women's World Cup and the Olympics in consecutive years.

73. Rhian Wilkinson, a two-time bronze medalist from Canada, said: "I think you don't get back-to-back winners because it takes different things to win those two tournaments."

74. Wilkinson might be onto something: the U.S. women's national team lost the 2023 Women's World Cup but won the 2024 Olympic gold.

75. That said, the United States holds the record for the most Olympic gold medals in women's soccer—five.

24 OLYMPIC MEDALS: WOMEN'S SOCCER

After the Women's World Cup, the Olympics is the second-most important women's international soccer tournament. The United States, Germany, Canada, and Norway have each earned gold medals in this event.

Year	Gold	Silver	Bronze
Paris 2024	United States	Brazil	Germany
Tokyo 2020	Canada	Sweden	United States
Rio 2016	Germany	Sweden	Canada
London 2012	United States	Japan	Canada
Beijing 2008	United States	Brazil	Germany
Athens 2004	United States	Brazil	Germany
Sydney 2000	Norway	United States	Germany
Atlanta 1996	United States	China	Norway

GAME CHANGER
Mia Hamm

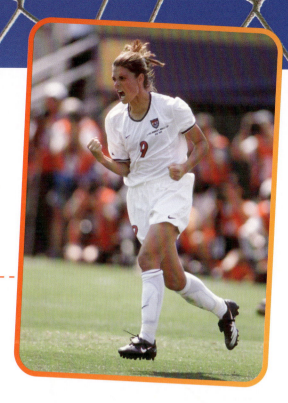

1. Mia Hamm earned two Women's World Cups and two Olympic gold medals in women's soccer. She competed—and triumphed—in the first ones ever held for women.

2. Mia Hamm, the fourth of six children, was born in 1972 in Selma, Alabama.

3. Until age two, Mia wore casts to correct a partial clubfoot.

4. Because her father was a U.S. Air Force fighter pilot, the family moved often. While living in Italy, young Mia discovered soccer.

5. She joined the U.S. women's national team in 1987 at the age of 15, scoring her first international goal at 18.

6. Mia Hamm played soccer at the University of North Carolina at Chapel Hill, where she won four NCAA championships. Her jersey number (19) was retired in 1994.

7. Hamm was named U.S. Soccer Player of the Year five times—a feat surpassed only by Abby Wambach.

8. The high-scoring forward was named FIFA Women's World Player of the Year in 2001 and 2002.

9. "What's hard is talking about myself," she said. "People throw out superlatives [about elite athletes]: 'You're the best. You're this. You're that.' And ever since I was little, I never felt that way."

10. Hamm became a co-owner of Los Angeles FC in the MLS in 2014 and helped launch the NWSL's Angel City FC in 2020. She is "proud to support the beautiful game."

38 FAST FACTS ABOUT FUTSAL

1. Futsal is an indoor version of soccer played on a hard court.

2. The game is quick and high-scoring.

3. You use your skills to control the ball and pass in small spaces in futsal.

4. Futsal originated in Uruguay in the 1930s.

5. *Futsal* is short for *fútbol sala* in Spanish and *futebol de salão* in Portuguese, which both mean "indoor football."

6. "During my childhood in Portugal, all we played was futsal," Cristiano Ronaldo said. "The small playing area helped me improve my close control, and when I played futsal, I felt free."

7. A futsal team has five players, including the goalkeeper.

8. A futsal ball (size 4) is smaller than a standard soccer ball (size 5).

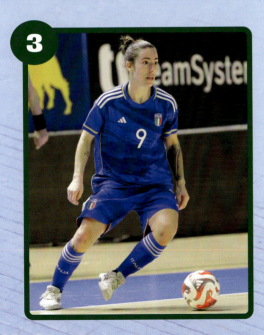

9. A futsal ball does not bounce as much as a standard soccer ball.

10. A futsal court is much smaller than a standard soccer field.

11. The goal measures 10 feet (3 meters) by 6.5 feet (2 meters).

12. There are no throw-ins in futsal.

13. The game uses kick-ins instead of throw-ins.

14. Kick-ins must be taken within four seconds.

15. Free kicks and corner kicks must be taken within four seconds.

16. The keeper must release the ball within four seconds.

17. All futsal players must wear a shirt with sleeves, shorts, and socks.

18. All futsal players must wear shin guards under their socks.

19. They must wear footwear with rubber soles.

20. Players may wear knee and arm protectors in futsal.

21. A futsal game lasts 40 minutes—two halves of 20 minutes.

22. The game clock stops whenever the ball is out of play or a foul is called.

23. Each team is permitted one time-out per half.

24. If needed, extra time is two five-minute periods, and then a penalty shootout decides the winner.

25. There is no offside in futsal.

26. You can be called for a handball offense in futsal.

27. Referees keep track of each team's fouls.

28. After a team has five fouls in one half, each additional foul gives the opposing team a free shot at goal.

29. Referees can give players yellow and red cards for fouls.

30. If a player earns a red card, they can be replaced on the court after a two-minute time penalty.

31. An unlimited number of substitutions is allowed in futsal.

32. If the ball hits the ceiling while in play, the game is restarted with a kick-in.

33. FIFA took over as the governing body of futsal in 1989.

34. The first edition of the FIFA Futsal World Cup took place in the Netherlands in 1989.

35. Sixteen teams participated in the sport's first World Cup. Brazil defeated the Netherlands in the final.

36. There are U.S. women's and men's national teams for futsal.

37. The FIFA Futsal Women's World Cup began in 2025.

38. Futsal is not yet an Olympic event.

38 SANDY FACTS ABOUT BEACH SOCCER

1. Beach soccer is played on sand. That makes sense.
2. Players must wear a shirt with sleeves to play beach soccer.
3. But they don't wear shoes or socks.
4. Players may wear knee and arm protectors in beach soccer.
5. Ankle guards for beach soccer are permitted too.
6. A beach soccer game lasts 36 minutes—three periods of 12 minutes.
7. There are no draws in beach soccer. (Three minutes of extra time, then a penalty shootout, if needed, decides the winner.)
8. Hands or feet are both permitted for throw-ins in beach soccer.
9. Using feet for a throw-in is called a kick-in.
10. A beach soccer field is much smaller than a standard soccer field.
11. Players can score from anywhere on the sand in beach soccer.

12. Even goalkeepers can score from their position in beach soccer.
13. Beach soccer is a fast-moving sport that rewards agility and skills in the air. The ball is in the air much of the time.
14. One beach soccer stat is "overhead kicks."
15. Land soccer and beach soccer use the same size ball.
16. A beach soccer ball is filled with less air than a standard soccer ball.
17. When you're playing on sand, a softer ball with less air in it is easier to handle.
18. In beach soccer, goals are scored every three or four minutes on average.
19. Law 11 of the official rules says: there is no offside in beach soccer.
20. But foul play can earn red and yellow cards.
21. Players can be called for a handball offense in beach soccer.

27

29. The first international beach soccer competitions took place in the 1990s.

30. FIFA took over as governing body of beach soccer in 2005.

31. Brazil hosted the first men's FIFA Beach Soccer World Cup in Rio de Janeiro in 2005.

32. Twelve teams participated in the sport's first World Cup. France defeated Portugal in the first final.

33. Pro soccer player and 1994 World Cup Golden Ball winner Romário played for Brazil at the first Beach Soccer World Cup.

34. There are U.S. men's and women's national teams for beach soccer.

35. U.S. Soccer established best Beach Soccer Player of the Year for men and women in 2021.

36. Antonio Chavez (3) and Hannah Adler were named U.S. Soccer Beach Soccer Players of the Year.

37. There hasn't been a women's Beach Soccer World Cup yet, but there are other international tournaments.

38. Beach soccer is not yet an Olympic event.

22. Free kicks in beach soccer must be taken by the player who was fouled.

23. You can't use a wall to block free kicks in beach soccer.

24. For international competition, the sand must be at least 40 centimeters (about 16 inches) deep.

25. A beach soccer team is made of five players, including the goalkeeper.

26. An unlimited number of substitutions is allowed in beach soccer.

27. Some say the sport originated in Brazil in the 19th century.

28. Beach soccer is sometimes called beasal, sand football, or beach footie.

36

32 FACTS ABOUT SOCCER GAMING

1. Sports video games simulate the practice of sports, either by playing or managing them.

2. You probably know the largest soccer video game franchise is *EA Sports FC* by Electronic Arts (EA).

3. More than 300 million copies of *EA Sports FC* have been sold over 30 years.

4. *EA Sports FC* used to be called *FIFA*. EA and FIFA's partnership ended with the release of *FIFA 23*.

5. *EA Sports FC* holds licenses for more than 19,000 players, 700 teams, and 30 different leagues. New versions are released every year.

6. Konami's *eFootball*, formerly *Pro Evolution Soccer*, has topped 800 million downloads worldwide.

7. The first soccer video games were created in the 1970s.

8. In the early 1990s, *Sensible World of Soccer* dominated soccer video gaming.

9. *Sensible World of Soccer* offered more than 1,500 clubs and 27,000 pro footballers.

10. In 1993, the first game in the FIFA series, *FIFA International Soccer*, was released.

11. The game featured national teams instead of club teams, and the players were not real people.

12. The biggest difference between early and later FIFA games was better graphics—and licensing.

13. *FIFA International Soccer* could not legally use player names or likenesses, team logos, or real stadiums.

14. *FIFA Soccer 95* had clubs from six European leagues.

15. *FIFA Soccer 96* introduced real-time three-dimensional graphics as well as player names and licenses.

16. *FIFA Soccer 03* allowed players to do tricks and feints for the first time.

17. In *FIFA Soccer 06*, players could manage a team over several seasons in so-called manager mode.

18. Before the 2015 Women's World Cup, 12 women's national teams were included in a FIFA video game, *FIFA 16*, for the first time.

19. Electronic Arts was the only officially licensed partner of the U.S. women's national team in 2017.

20. Women's professional clubs were included in a FIFA video game for the first time in 2023.

21. Wayne Rooney of England and Ronaldinho were the FIFA video game cover athletes from 2006 to 2009.

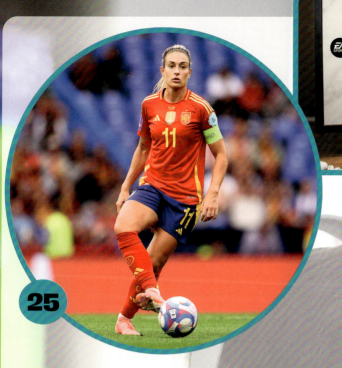

22. Kylian Mbappé was the FIFA cover star from 2021 to 2023.

23. Sam Kerr was the first woman player featured on a FIFA global video game cover, in 2023.

24. Jude Bellingham appeared on the *EA Sports FC 25* cover, after Erling Haaland in 2024.

25. Alexia Putellas, with four-star skill moves and a five-star weak foot, was the third-best player in *FC 25*. One and two were Mbappé and Rodri.

26. Soccer matches in the *EA Sports FC* video game now take place in more than 120 real-life stadiums.

27. After scoring, you can also choose to celebrate with a funky walk, a pigeon move, or a chicken dance.

28. Soccer video games have been used to research decision-making and reaction times.

29. The longest video-game marathon playing a soccer game was set in 2024. It lasted 100 hours and 7 minutes.

30. The esports tournament FIFAe World Cup attracts thousands of players—and millions of viewers—every year.

31. Virtual soccer leagues with digital players could one day replace real-live football on the pitch.

32. But probably not.

WHAT ARE SOME **TIPS AND TRICKS**?
24 EXCELLENT ANSWERS FROM **SOCCER PROS**

1. "If you ever want to be a decent player, you have to be able to use each foot equally without stopping to think about it." **Pelé (Forward)**

2. "[How did I develop my skills?] Everyday playing with my friends. Watching clips on YouTube of Neymar skills. And then copy." **Xavi Simons (Midfielder)**

3. "Practice against a wall." **Christian Eriksen (Midfielder)**

4. "Make mistakes." **Becky Sauerbrunn (Defender)**

5. "Dribble around cones. Set a time, and then try to do it first in 15 seconds, then in 10 seconds. Try to do it as quickly as possible. The ball cannot touch the cones." **Bernardo Silva (Midfielder)**

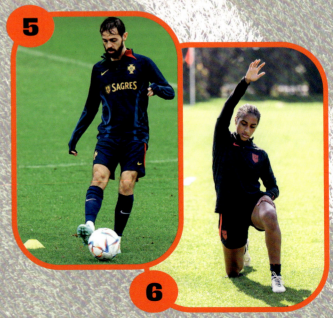

6. "Stretch, do a few jogs, skip. But I also try to warm up mentally by making sure that I am ready for drills during the session and making sure that I am ready to perform and find spaces during training." **Naomi Girma (Defender)**

7. "Just plain repetition shooting. It's very important to get your confidence up to get the right technique." **Christine Sinclair (Forward)**

8. "It's important to be fast, to be quick, to be strong, but the most important is to be smart, to be clever." **Cristiano Ronaldo (Forward)**

9. "Watch a lot of soccer." **Alex Morgan (Forward)**

10. "Juggling is really important because it prepares you for the big moment in a game, when you need to bring down a ball that's in the air and score a goal for your team." **Christen Press (Forward)**

11. "Even if you're extremely athletic and fast, if you're doing the same thing over and over, the defense is going to figure it out. Really, it's all about playing cat-and-mouse with the defender so I try to change it up and put [myself] in a position where [I] have options." **Megan Rapinoe (Midfielder)**

12. "Don't press straight on, because all the player on the ball has to do is take a touch and all you can do is foul them. You always need to press at a certain angle and try to predict which way they are going to go." **Tyler Adams (Midfielder)**

13. "Before you receive the ball, know what you want to do. That's for me the most important thing." **Xavi Simons (Midfielder)**

14. "It's not about just the last ball; it's about the whole game. I'm not looking just one time before I get the ball, I look a lot of times before. Maybe before the the ball is there, I look. Then the ball gets here and I look again. I look all the time." **Martin Odegaard (Midfielder)**

15. "In football, you need players with the ball, and also you need players without the ball—they make their runs, they make the right decisions." **Thomas Müller (Midfielder)**

16. "As a center back, you have the overview and you have to try to organize what's in front of you, what's around you, and lead by example." **Virgil van Dijk (Defender)**

17. "As a midfielder, the toughest part is when we *don't* have the ball, figuring out why the opposition is getting the better of us—and looking for a solution to prevent that." **Alexia Putellas (Midfielder)**

18. "I'm always about goals. Being in the right position to score a goal." **Khadija "Bunny" Shaw (Forward)**

19. "It's about getting to the ball as efficiently as possible to generate the power in the moment and afterwards. Where does the ball go after that? Sometimes people forget that. I know there's a player at the back post so I'm trying to parry it into an area where she can't just tap it in." **Mary Earps (Goalkeeper)**

19

20. "I try to do breathing exercises now and then in the evenings and get into a nice, calming state." **Virgil van Dijk (Defender)**

21. "I've always fallen back on my preparation. Every detail matters. If I can prepare the way that I want to prepare, then I can feel good and comfortable going into a game and confident." **Alyssa Naeher (Goalkeeper)**

22. "[What are you drinking?] It's water. Nothing secret. I just like to have my own bottle." **Marta (Forward)**

23. "Since I was young I just wanted to be on the field. Being able to adapt my game and show coaches I was able to play in multiple positions gave me the best opportunity to be on the field." **Tyler Adams (Midfielder)**

24. "Live in the moment. Don't look too far forward or too far back and just be present." **Sophia Wilson (Forward)**

24

INDEX

Page numbers in **bold** indicate a key reference.

A

Aarones, Ann Kristin, 71, 150
ACL (anterior cruciate ligament) tears, 77
Acosta, Kellyn, 128
Acosta, Luciano, 97
Adams, Tyler, 49, 80, 122, 170, 197, 199
added time, 56
additional time, 56
Ademir, 134
Adidas, 45
Adler, Hannah, 193
advice for young players, 8, 40, 41, 43, 53, 80–81, 120, 135, 153, 196–199
AFC (Asian Football Confederation), 101, 102, 104, 106–111, 112–117
Afif, Akram, 102
Ajax, 133, 161
Akers, Michelle, 22, 23, 24, **25**, 39, 71, 117, 144, 150
Alber, Mara, 155
Albert, Flórián, 134, 138
Albert, Korbin, 155
Algeria, 53, 105, 165
Allen, Amanda, 155
Al-Nassr FC, 179
Altidore, Jozy, 128, 171

American football, 12, 25, 118, 135, 164
American Indian game, 7
Amoros, Manuel, 138
ancient cultures, 6, 75, 93
Andrade, José Leandro, 17
Angerer, Nadine, 42, 152, 180
Antarctica, 100
Argentina, 13, 34, 35, 36, 54, 55, 67, 91, 96, **106**, 109, **112**, 132, 134, 136, 138, 163, 178
    1930 World Cup, 15–18
    2022 World Cup, 30–32, 51, 164, 166
    in the MLS, 169, 170
    at the Olympics, 184, 185, 186
arms factory, 21, 137
Aspin, Brooke, 155
assistant referees, 62, 63, 49
"association football," 12
Aston, Ken, 50
Atlanta, Georgia, 98, 171, 176, 183, 184, 188
Atubolu, Noah, 139
Australia, 70, 102, **106**, 112, 115, 154, 155, 156, 157, 174, 180
    2023 Women's World Cup, 37, 63, 76, 95, 166

Austria, 105, 111, 184
Azteca Stadium, 109

B
backflip celebration, 70
backheel kick, 55
back-pass violation, 60
Baggio, Roberto, 34, 80
Baleba, Carlos Noom Quomah, 139
ballet, 153
Ballon d'Or, 34, 89, 103, 127, 133, 137
Ballon d'Or Féminin, 89, 149, 151, 179
Ballon d'Or Women's Soccer Coach of the Year, 41
Balogun, Folarin, 122
Banda, Barbra, 101, 102, 117, 176
Barbie dolls, 97
Bardghji, Roony, 139
Barthez, Fabien, 136
baseball, 12, 97, 119
basketball, 12, 45, 80, 118, 149, 183
Batistuta, Gabriel, 67
BC Place, 38
beach soccer, 7, 13, **192–193**
Beasley, DaMarcus, 5, 66, 128
"beautiful game," 19
Bebeto (José Roberto Gama de Oliveira), 65
Beckenbauer, Franz, 138
Beckham, David, 100, 135, 169
Beckham rule, 169
Belgium, 13, 15, **106**, 130, 136, 138, 140, 143, 164, 178, 184
Bellingham, Jude, 9, 80, 87, 139, 143, 195
Ben Seghir, Eliesse, 139
Benzema, Karim, 178
Benzina, Nouhaila, 47
Bergvall, Lucas, 139
Berhalter, Gregg, 129
Bethune, Croix, 174
bicycle kick, 55
Biyendolo, Lynn (formerly Williams), 173
Bledsoe, Aubrey (formerly Kingsbury), 176
blue card, 52
bobbleheads, 96
Bolivia, 15
Bonmatí, Aitana, 42, 89, 148, **149**, 180
boots, 10, 70, 96, 134, 150
Borussia Dortmund, 59
Boston, Massachusetts, 45, 69, 98, 173
brace, 10, 158, 160
Bradley, Michael, 129
Brazil, 4, 15, 19, 27, 34, 36, 37, 42, 43, 48, 55, 65, 67, 71, 74, 76, 94, 98, 99, 103, 104, **106**, 107, **112**, 116, 120, 132, 134, 138, 140, 141, 142, 148, 150, 156, 157, 160, 167, 169, 174, 178, 180, 191, 193
   1991 Women's World Cup, 23, 24
   2011 Women's World Cup, 51, 145, 147
   at the Olympics, 21, 183, 184, 185, 186, 187, 188
breakfast cereal, 25, 97
breathing techniques, 119, 120, 199
British Ladies Football Club, 21
broadcasting deals, 12, 163, 164, 175
Bronze, Lucy, 42, 81
Brooks, John, 129
Buchanan, Kadeisha, 154
Buehler, Rachel, 51
Buenos Aires, Argentina, 8, 33, 64, 103, 106, 112, 140
Buffon, Gianluigi, 73, 136
Bulgaria, 134, 184
Bundesliga, 139, 164, 169
Burkina Faso, 142

C
Cabrini, Antonio, 138
CAF (Confederation of African Football), 101, 102, 106–111, 112–117
Caicedo, Linda, 113, 155
Cambridge University, 8

Camello, Sergio, 186
Cameroon, **107**, 110, 139, 184, 186
Canada, 8, 13, 22, 37, 71, 94, 98, 100, 103, 104, **107**, **112**, 154, 155, 160, 162, 166
    in the MLS, 168, 170
    at the Olympics, 184, 187, 188
Canadian Soccer Federation, 103
Cannavaro, Fabio, 34
cap, 10
Capeta, Ana, 116
Cape Town, South Africa, 8
captain (national team), 49, 54
carb rinsing, 88
Carmona, Olga, 116
Carrasquilla, Adalberto, 103
Casillas, Iker, 73, 136
Castro, Hector, 17
Cea, Pedro, 17
center mark, 54
chances of scoring a penalty kick, 58
changing sides at halftime, 86
Chastain, Brandi, 23, 68, 144
Chavez, Antonio, 193
Chawinga, Temwa, 173, 174
Chelsea FC, 41, 59, 85, 181
Chile, 13, 15, 36, 74, 134, 184
China, 6, 7, 25, 37, 71, 92, 93, **113**, 148, 150, 152, 166
    1999 Women's World Cup, 22, 23, 24
    at the Olympics, 183, 188
Chinese Taipei, 23, 24, 115
chippy, 46
clean sheet, 11, 72, 130, 131, 136, 137, 146, 147, 152
Clegg, Milly, 155
Codina, Laia, 74
coaches, 8, 11, 22, 23, 24, 25, 33, 41, 49, 52, 70, 83, 120, 129, 133, 144, 160, 170, 181, 186, 187, 199
    highest paid, 163

Coffey, Sam, 120, 122
coin toss, 49, 54, 57
Coll, Cata, 72
Colombia, 65, 83, 101, **113**, 116, 134, 140, 155, 157, 169
CONCACAF (Confederation of North, Central America and Caribbean Association Football), 100, 103, 104, 107, 109, 111, 112–117, 127, 140, 170
concussions, 78
CONMEBOL (South American Football Confederation), 101, 103, 104, 106, 107, 111, 112, 113, 142
cooling breaks, 48
Cooper, Michelle, 174
corner kick, 54, 55, 61, 88, 190
Costa Rica, 63, **107**, **113**, 117, 141, 156, 159
Côte d'Ivoire, 65, 143
Courtois, Thibaut, 136
Cowell, Cade, 140
CPKC Stadium, 173
cricket, 11, 46, 47, 182
Cristiane, 71, 183, 186
Croatia, 34, 36, 49, 59, **107**, 132, 134, 140, 157, 168, 179
Cruyff, Johan, 81, **133**
Cruz, Shirley, 159
Cubarsí, Pau, 140
Cubillas, Teófilo, 67, 138
Czechoslovakia, 26, 36, 134, 184

D

Dallas, Texas, 98, 171
Darke, Ian (TV commentator), 165
Davidson, Tierna, 122
Davies, Alphonso, 168
Debinha, 176
De Bruyne, Kevin, 164, 178
Dembélé, Ousmane, 30, 31
Dempsey, Clint, 5, 66, 72, 128, 129
Denmark, 13, 22, 23, 97, **107**, **113**, 139, 144, 158, 182, 183, 184

Dest, Sergiño, 123
Diallo, Hapsatou Malado, 155
DiCicco, Tony, 25
Dick, Kerr Ladies club, 21
digital collectibles, 97
Di María, Ángel, 30, 31, 186
Diouf, Amara, 140
direct kick, 54
distance covered in a match, 118
Dominican Republic, 158
Donovan, Landon, 5, 120, 128, 129, 138, **165**, 171, 185
Dorado, Pablo, 17
Dorrance, Anson, 23, 24
Doué, Désiré, 140
Dragoni, Giulia, 155
dribbling, 9, 59, 196
drones, 98
Dudinha, 156
Dumornay, Melchie, 103, 156
Dunn, Crystal, 123, 173, 174, 180
Durán, Jhon, 140

E

Earps, Mary, 152, **153**, 198
EA Sports FC, 194, 195
East Germany, 184
East Rutherford, New Jersey, 98
Ebi, Onome, 187
Echeverri, Claudio, 140
Ecuador, **107**, 117, 142
eFootball, 194
Egypt, 15, 102, 119, 178
electronic board, 57, 62
Electronic performance and tracking systems (EPTS), 48
El Khannouss, Bilal, 140
Enderby, Mia, 156
endorsements, 25, 175, 178, 180
Endrick, 140
England, 3, 13, 20, 21, 36, 37, 38, 41, 42, 45, 46, 50, 55, 59, 67, 69, 70, 72, 79, 83, 87, **108**, **113**, 120, 122, 124, 125, 134, 135, 138, 139, 141, 142, 152, 153, 155, 156, 158, 163, 164, 168, 169, 180, 181, 182, 194
   1930 World Cup, 14, 18
   1966 World Cup, 26, 27, 31, 33, 90, 96
   2022 World Cup, 3
   history of soccer, 7, 8, 9, 10
equal pay, 121, 151
Equatorial Guinea, 143
Eritrea, 161
Ertz, Julie (formerly Johnston), 39, 145
Estadio Centenario, 17
Estêvão, 140
Ethiopia, 123, 181
Eusébio, 134
excessive force, 48, 49, 50
extra time, 57

F

fans, 8, 18, 29, 82–85, 86, 90–95, 96–97, 98–99, 120
fastest soccer players, 119, 140
Fawcett, Joy, 23
Fazer, Laurina, 156
feinting, 48, 61, 194
Ferreira, Manuel, 17
field of play, 48
FIFA
   2015 Women's World Cup final, 38–40
   2022 World Cup final, 30–32
   Best FIFA Men's Players, 34
   Best FIFA Women's Players, 42
   Club World Cup, 164, 170
   confederations, 100–104
   facts and figures, 12–13, 162–164
   first Women's World Cup, 22–24
   first World Cup, 2, 14–18
   founding nations, 13
   Golden Ball winners (men), 132
   Golden Ball winners (women), 148
   Golden Boot winners (men), 134

Golden Boot winners (women), 150
Golden Glove winners (men), 136
Golden Glove winners (women), 152
headquarters, 12
history of trophies, 26–29
museum, 27
nations that competed at the 2022 World Cup, 106–111
nations that competed at the 2023 Women's World Cup, 112–117
paying clubs to release players, 164
Technical Study Group, 132, 136, 138, 148, 152, 154
top all-time World Cup goal scorers (men), 67
top all-time World Cup goal scorers (women), 71
trophies, 26–29
Women's Coach of the Year, 41
Women's World Cup champions list, 37
World Cup ball designs, 45, 73, 74–76
World Cup champions list, 36
World Cup draw, 105
World Cup mascots, 3, 90–95, 96
World Cup prize pools, 166–167
World Cup qualifying tables, 104
World Cup Winner's Trophies, 28, 29
world rankings, 106
Young Player Awards (men), 138
Young Player Awards (women), 154
FIFAe World Cup, 195
Figo, Luís, 34
first U.S. football club, 45
first women's football match, 20
flags
    buzzer or beep, 62
    corner, 66
    national, 75, 87, 83, 84, 91, 92, 106–111, 112–117
flopping, 11

Florie, Tom, 16
Foden, Phil, 9
Fontaine, Just, 67, 80, 134
Foord, Caitlin, 154
Football Association, the, 7, 8
    banning women, 20, 21
Forbes, 178, 180
Forlán, Diego, 73, 132
Formiga, 4, 186
Foudy, Julie, 23, 81, 145, 172
fouls, 9, 11, 49, 50–52, 54–55, 62, 80, 191, 192, 197
fourth official, 62, 63
Fowler, Mary, 156
Fox, Emily, 123, 174
France, 12, 13, 26, 34, 36, 37, 49, 52, 53, 63, 67, 69, 73, 74, 75, 85, 92, 95, **108**, **113**, 132, 134, 136, 138, 139, 140, 142, 143, 151, 156, 157, 166, 167, 169, 178, 193
    1930 World Cup, 15, 16
    2022 World Cup, 30, 31, 64, 164
    at the Olympics, 184, 186
France Football, 41, 89, 103
Frappart, Stéphanie, 63
free agency, 175
Friedel, Brad, 130
friendly, 48
Fujino, Aoba, 156
futsal, 13, **190–191**

G

Galic, Daniela, 157
game clock, 3, 24, 56, 57, 60, 87, 191
Gandhi, Mahatma, 8
Garrincha, 134
Gaupset, Signe, 157
George, Finidi, 65
Germany, 13, 27, 29, 32, 34, 36, 37, 38, 40, 42, 59, 67, 71, 75, 76, 85, 90, 93, 94, 96, 103, 105, **108**, 110, 113, **114**, 116, 119, 129, 130, 132, 134, 136, 138,

Germany (cont.), 139, 142, 143, 148, 150, 152, 153, 154, 155, 164, 169, 180
    1991 Women's World Cup, 23, 24
    2022 World Cup, 63, 141
    at the Olympics, 184, 185, 186, 188
    World Cup prize pools, 166, 167
Ghana, 66, **108**, 119, 124, 129, 184
Gill, Adrian, 140
Girma, Naomi, 81, 120, 123, 145, 174, **181**, 187, 196
Giroud, Olivier, 31, 186
Glasgow Herald, 20
goal celebrations, 31, 35, 51, 56, 64–66, 68–70, 87, 121, 158, 195
goal differential, 16, 105
goalkeeper facts, 60–61
goalkeeper gloves, 60, 72
goalkeepers, 72, 73, 80, 127, 130, 131, 136, 137, 139, 141, 142, 146, 147, 152, 153, 158, 198, 199
goal kick, 54, 88
Goal Line Technology (GLT), 48
Gomes, Aline, 157
Goodyear, Charles, 44, 45
Götze, Mario, 96
Grealish, Jack, 46
Great Britain, 7, 8, 13, 21, 69, 90, 100, 182, 184, 186
Great Depression, 15
Greece, 6, 26, 46, 65, 83
Green, Robert, 72
Group of Death, 105
group stage, 105, 183
Guadalajara, Mexico, 98
Guardiola, Pep, 149, 163
Guilherme, Luis, 140
Güler, Arda, 141
Guyana, 100
Guzmán, Ana María, 157
Gwinn, Giulia, 154

H

Haaland, Erling, 81, 164, 178, 195
Haiti, 103, **114**, 156, 157
Hamano, Maika, 157
Hamm, Mia, 23, 42, 80, 145, 172, 186, **189**
"hand of God" goal, 33, 96
Harder, Pernille, 113
Hato, Jorrel, 141
hat trick, 10, 16, 24, 31, 39, 64, 96, 113, 117, 185
Hayes, Emma, **41**, 163, 181
headbutting, 52
heading the ball, 44, 45, 78
Heaps, Lindsey (formerly Horan), 80, 124, 173, 176
Heath, Tobin, 39, 176
heat stress, 79
Hegerberg, Ada, 180
Heinrichs, April, 23, 24
Henrique, Luiz, 103
Henry, Lori, 22, 23
Henry, Thierry, 80, 169, 186
Heung-min, Son, 81, 101
highest-paid men's soccer players, 178
highest-paid women's soccer players, 180
hijab, 47
hip-hop music, 65, 81
hogs' heads, 6
holding offense, 48
holes in soccer socks, 87
Holiday, Jrue, 145
Holiday, Lauren, 39, 145, 172, 176
Honeyball, Nettie J., **21**
Hong, Gao, 152
Houston, Texas, 98, 171, 172
Howard, Tim, 5, 130
Humm, Fabienne, 117
Hungary, 26, 36, 67, 134, 138, 183, 184, 186
Hurst, Geoff, 31, 96
Hutton, Claire, 157
hydration, 48, 79, 118

I

Ibrahimovic, Zlatan, 169
ice baths, 79
India, 8
indirect kick, 54, 61
injuries, 3, 11, 25, 41, 46, 49, 56, 77–79, 87, 115
injury time, 56
International Football Association Board (IFAB), 7
Iran, 3, **108**, 139
Iraq, 157
Iriarte, Santos, 44
Italy, 13, 26, 27, 28, 34, 36, 52, 65, 73, 74, 78, 91, 108, 110, **114**, 116, 124, 132, 134, 135, 136, 138, 155, 164, 167, 169, 184, 189
    1930 World Cup, 14, 15
    1991 Women's World Cup, 22, 23
Ivanov, Valentin, 134

J

Jabulani ball, 73, 76
Jamaica, 114, 155
Japan, 6, 36, 37, 42, 70, 75, 84, 93, 101, 102, **108**, **114**, 116, 128, 140, 140, 148, 150, 156, 157, 158, 160, 167
    1991 Women's World Cup, 23, 24
    2015 Women's World Cup, 38, 39
    at the Olympics, 184, 185, 187, 188
Jennings, Carin, 23, 24, 148
Jerkovic, Drazan, 134
Jones, Cobi, 129, 130
Jones, Jermaine, 130
Jordan, 142
Jordan, Michael, 183
Joseph, Liana, 157
Joveljic, Dejan, 170
juggling, 197
Juventus, 179

K

Kafaji, Rosa, 157
Kahn, Oliver, 132, 136
Kaihori, Ayumi, 38, 84

Kaká, 34
Kane, Harry, 9, 134, **135**
Kansas City, Missouri, 98, 171, 173, 174, 176
Kaptein, Wieke, 157
Keating, Khiara, 158
Keller, Kasey, 130
Kelly, Chloe, 55
kemari, 6
Kempes, Mario, 134
Kerolin, 174
Kerr, Sam, 70, 174, 180, 195
kickoff, 54
Kiowa tribe, 170
klaphat, 82
Klinsmann, Jürgen, 67
Klose, Miroslav, 69, 134
knockout stage, 105, 183
Kochen, Diego, 141
Kocsis, Sándor, 67, 134
Koga, Toko, 158
Krieger, Ali, 145
Kühl, Kathrine, 158
Kuwait, 139, 185

L

Lalas, Alexi, 5, 131
La Liga, 163, 164, 169
Lato, Grzegorz, 67, 134
Laurent, Lucien, 16
Lavelle, Rose, 96, 124, 173, 174
Laws of the Game, the, 7, 62
Liga F, 180
Leônidas, 134
Lewandowski, Robert, 34, 109
Lewis, Rico, 141
LGBTQ rights, 151
Liberia, 34, 127
Lilly, Kristine, 23, 146, 172
Lineker, Gary, 67, 134
Lloris, Hugo, 30, 31, 73
Lloyd, Carli, 5, 38, 39, 40, 42, 71, 146, 148

London, England, 7, 21, 26, 41, 122, 124, 135, 153, 184
longest video-game marathon, 195
Lookman, Ademola, 102
López, Fermín, 186
López, Vicky, 158
Los Angeles, California, 98, 165, 168, 170, 171, 172, 176, 184, 189
Luna, Diego, 170
Luvanga, Clara, 158

M

M&M's, 23
Macario, Catarina, 77
Mainoo, Kobbie, 141
Major League Soccer (MLS)
    history, 168–170
        MLS Cup champions and challengers, 171
        MLS Supporters' Shield, 170
Manchester City (club), 59, 140, 159, 163
Manchester United, 59, 83, 179
Mandela, Nelson, 28
Mané, Sadio, 178
Maracanã Stadium, 99
Maradona, Diego, 32, **33**, 96, 132
Marta, 42, **43**, 51, 71, 148, 150, 172, 176, 180, 186, 187, 199
Martens, Lieke, 42
Martínez, Emiliano, 32, 136
Mary, Queen of Scots, 44
mascots, 3, 90–95, 96
match report, 49
Matthäus, Lothar, 34
Mbappé, Kylian, 30, 31, 32, 64, 67, 134, 138, 178, 185, 195
McDonald, Jessica, 176
McKennie, Weston, 81, 124, 170
Medalen, Linda, 24, 71
meditation, 119, 120, 199
memorable quotes, 80–81
Meola, Tony, 131, 171

Messi, Lionel, 30, 31, 32, 34, **35**, 51, 53, 55, 67, 89, 97, 129, 132, 141, 169, 178, 185, 186
Mewis, Kristie, 159
Mewis, Sam, 159
Mexican Football Federation, 103
Mexico, 6, 22, 36, 50, 75, 82, 90, 91, 98, 100, 103, 104, **109**, 160, 162, 167, 184, 185
    1930 World Cup, 15, 16
Mexico City, 98, 103, 109, 184
Miami, Florida, 98, 169
Michels, Rinus, 133
Miedema, Vivianne, 115
Miley, Lewis, 141
mindfulness, 120, 199
missing a penalty kick, 58
mistakes, 72–73, 133, 141, 196
Mittag, Anja, 186
Miyazawa, Hinata, 150
Modric, Luka, 34, 81, 132
Mohr, Heidi, 71
Monterrey, Mexico, 98
Montiel, Gonzalo, 32
Moore, Bobby, 27
Morace, Carolina, 155
Morgan, Alex, 47, 69, 71, 97, 117, 120, **121**, 146, 158, 180, 197
Morocco, 47, **109**, 110, **114**, 139, 140, 143, 184
Morris, Jordan, 97
Moscardo, Gabriel, 141
Moultrie, Olivia, 158, 174
Mourinho, José, 11, 85
Müller, Gerd, 67, 134
Müller, Thomas, 67, 134, 138, 198
Mundialito ("Little World Cup"), 22
Musah, Yunus, 124
muscle strain, 48, 79, 87, 118
Musiala, Jamal, 141

N

Naeher, Alyssa, 61, 146, 187, 199
Naismith, James, 45
name, image, and likeness (NIL), 175, 194
Nasazzi, José, 17
National Football Hall of Fame (Manchester, England), 21
National Football Museum (Manchester, England), 27
National Soccer Hall of Fame (Frisco, Texas), 29
National Women's Soccer League (NWSL)
    Challenge Cup, 174, 175
    champions and challengers, 176
    championship, 122, 174, 175, 177
    draft, 126, 174, 175, 177, 181
    history, 172–175
    investors, 175
    NWSL Shield, 174
    SheBelieves Cup, 157, 160
NCAA, 25, 181, 189
Neid, Silvia, 24
Nejedly, Oldrich, 134
Netherlands, 13, 14, 34, 36, 37, 42, 51, 65, 82, **109**, **115**, 123, 133, 138, 141, 142, 152, 157, 161, 184, 191
    2019 Women's World Cup, 63, 69, 124
Neuer, Manuel, 80, 136, 139
New York City, 19, 29, 85, 122, 124, 172
"New York New Jersey Stadium," 99
New York Times, 8
New Zealand, 23, 37, 63, 76, 95, 103, 107, 112, **115**, 155, 166
Neymar, 178, 185, 196
nicknames
    players, 19, 59, 125, 129, 130, 137, 140, 187
    teams, 112, 108, 114
Nigeria, 23, 55, 65, 102, **115**, 116, 122, 139, 157, 184, 186, 187
Nighswonger, Jenna, 174
Nike, 26, 163, 175
North American Soccer League, 19
North Korea, 109
Northern Ireland, 108, 182
Norway, 22, 23, 24, 29, 37, 71, 72, **115**, 116, 142, 148, 150, 157, 164, 178, 180, 184, 186, 188
number 10, 35
number 13, 158
number 19, 189
Nusa, Antonio, 142
nutmegging, 10, 92
nutrition, 81, 118

O

Oceania, 15, 100, 101, 102, 103, 104, 115
Odegaard, Martin, 198
OFC (Oceania Football Confederation) 101, 103, 104, 115
offside rule, 31, 56, 62, 191, 192
oldest soccer ball in the world, 44
Olympic soccer, 182–188
    men's medals, 184
    women's medals, 188
olympicos, 55
Onzari, Cesáreo, 54
orange card, 80
O'Reilly, Heather, 146, 176
origins of football (soccer), 6–9
Ortega, Sara, 158
Ouédraogo, Assan, 142
Overbeck, Carla, 23
Overmars, Marc, 138
Owen, Michael, 138
own goals, 39, 57, 72–73

P

Páez, Kendry, 142
Panama, 103, **115**, 125
pandemic, 85, 177
Paraguay, 15, 16, 18, 109, 184
Paralluelo, Salma, 154, 159

Paredes, Kevin, 142
Paris, France, 12, 85, 182, 184, 189
Paris Saint-Germain FC, 156
"parking the bus," 11
Parr, Lily, **21**
pasuckquakkohowog, 7
Patenaude, Bert, 16
Pearce, Christine (formerly Rampone), 146, 186
Pékérman, José, 83
Pelé (Edson Arantes do Nascimento), **19**, 32, 33, 67, 96, 138, 183, 196
penalty kick, 55
penalty kick rules and strategies, 48, 51, 58, 61
penalty shootout rules and strategies, 57, 58, 120
Pepi, Ricardo, 142, 170
Perisic, Ivan, 49
Peru, 15, 16, 67, 138, 141
petroleum jelly, 60
pets, 47, 98
Peucelle, Carlos, 17
Pfeiffer, Alex, 159
Phair, Casey Yu-jin, 159
Philadelphia, Pennsylvania, 98, 143, 171, 176
Philippines, 102, **115**
physical fitness, 118, 119
Pickles (dog), 26, 27
pig's bladder, 44
player escorts, 86
playing a man down, 51
PlayStation, 64, 79, 177
Pochettino, Mauricio, 163
Podolski, Lukas, 138
Pogba, Paul, 138
Poland, 34, 67, **109**, 134, 138, 184
Portugal, 11, 34, **109**, **116**, 130, 134, 178, 179, 190, 193
practicing skills, 196–199
Première Ligue, 180

Premier League, 85, 135, 142, 143, 164, 168, 169
Press, Christen, 197
Preud'homme, Michel, 136
pre-wrap, 47
Prinz, Birgit, 42, 71, 148, 150, 176
promising attacks, 50, 63
Prosinecki, Roberto, 138
Pulisic, Christian, **59**, 80, 124, 185
Purce, Midge, 176
Putellas, Alexia, 42, 180, 195, 198

Q

Qatar, 3, 30, 36, 63, 76, 95, 98, 102, 106, **109**, 162, 164, 167
Queen Elizabeth, 27
quick passes, 133, 149

R

racial justice, 151
racism, 8, 53
Rahn, Helmut, 67
ransom note, 26
Rapinoe, Megan, 38, 42, 55, 69, 71, 80, 89, 147, 148, 150, **151**, 197
Raum, David, 119
rattles, 83
Real Madrid, 53, 59, 83, 179
Ream, Tim, 124
reckless plays, 49, 50
recovery, 118
red cards, 50–52, 62, 80, 191, 192
Redondo, Federico, 170
refereeing facts, 50–52, 56–57, 62–63
ref-player communication, 63
regulation time, 56
removing jersey, 51
Republic of Ireland, **116**
reserve kits, 47
Restes, Guillaume, 142
Reyna, Claudio, 125, 131
Reyna, Gio, 125, 131
Richards, Chris, 125
Richarlison, 55, 185

Riise, Hege, 71, 148, 186
Rimet, Jules, 18, 26
Rio de Janeiro, Brazil, 15, 27, 99, 193
Rivaldo, 34
Robinson, Antonee, 119, 125
Rodman, Trinity, 81, 97, 126, 160, **177**, 187
Rodman, Dennis, 126, 177
Rodri, 77, 164, 195
Rodriguez, Amy, 176
Rodríguez, James, 65, 134
Rodríguez, Raquel "Rocky," 113
Romania, 15, 16
Romário, 34, 65, 132, 192
Rome, Italy, 13, 184
Ronaldinho, 34, 35, 81, 194
Ronaldo, 34, 67, 132, 134
Ronaldo, Cristiano, 34, 89, 155, 178, **179**, 190, 197
Rooney, Wayne, 135, 169, 170, 194
Roque, Vitor, 142
rosettes, 83
Rossi, Paolo, 132
roster, 49
Rottenberg, Silke, 152
Round of 16, 105
round robin, 105
rugby, 45
Russia, 36, 95, 134, 135, 136, 137, 167

Salah, Mohamed, 119, 178
salary cap, 169
Salenko, Oleg, 134
Sánchez, Leonel, 134
Sánchez, María, 180
San Francisco, California, 98
SARS illness, 93
Sasic, Célia, 40, 150
Saudi Arabia, **110**
Sauerbrunn, Becky, 147, 196
Sawa, Homare, 42, 148, 150, 187
scarves, 83

Schillaci, Salvatore, 132, 134
Scifo, Enzo, 138
Scotland, 7, 8, 9, 20, 44, 79, 108, 182
Scott, Sheika, 159
Scurry, Briana, 78, 147, 152
Seattle, Washington, 25, 98, 131, 151, 171, 172, 176
Seike, Kiko, 102
Senegal, **110**, 140, 155, 178
Sentnor, Ally, 159, 174
Serbia, 55, **110**, 170
Serie A, 164, 169
serious foul play, 49
set pieces, 88
Shakespeare, William, 7
Shakira, 65
Shaw, Jaedyn, 126, 155, 159, 174
Shaw, Khadija "Bunny," 198
shin guards, 46–47
shirts (jerseys), 5, 9, 10, 20, 46–47, 51, 60, 68, 96, 97, 163, 190, 192
    retired jerseys, 189, 172
    swapping jerseys, 53, 89
shoebox, 26
Silva, Bernardo, 196
Simeone, Diego, 163
Simons, Xavi, 142, 196, 197
simulation, 49, 51
Sinclair, Christine, 71, 112, 147, 176, 187, 197
Sissi, 150
six-second rule, 60, 61
sleep, 81, 118
Smith, Kelly, 70
snow angels, 121
soccer ball rules and history, 44–45
    official requirements, 44
Soccer City, 99
soccer drills, 196, 197,
soccer gaming, 194–195
soccer jargon and terms, 10–11, 48–49
soccer kicks, 54–55

soccer swag, 96–97
soccer traditions, 82–85, 86–89
socks, 10, 46–47, 87, 190, 192
Solo, Hope, 38, 40, 147, 152
Soma, Pedro, 142
Sonnett, Emily, 174
Soto, Alice, 160
South Africa, 8, 13, 28, 36, 66, 72, 76, 83, 94, 99, **116**, 167
South Korea, 36, 75, 93, 101, **110**, **116**, 130, 155, 159, 167, 184
Soviet Union, 134, 137, 184
Spain, 13, 35, 36, 37, 42, 53, 73, 77, 83, 91, 97, 103, 109, **110**, 114, **116**, 119, 136, 140, 141, 143, 148, 149, 154, 155, 156, 158, 159, 166, 167, 180, 185
    1930 World Cup, 14, 15
    2023 Women's World Cup, 72, 113, 116, 153
    at the Olympics, 184, 186
spin turns, 53
spitting, 52, 88
Sports Illustrated, 68, 69
Stábile, Guillermo, 16, 17, 134
stadiums, 14, 16, 17, 21, 24, 27, 30, 38, 48, 83, 98–99, 109, 162, 185, 194, 195
starting lineup, 49
St Clair, Lily, 20
Stoichkov, Hristo, 134
stolen trophies, 26–29
stoppage time, 56
St. Peter's Basilica, 13
stress, 58, 63, 199, 120, 177
Suárez, Luis, 97, 108
substitutions, 3, 9, 49, 52, 56, 63, 129, 141, 191, 193
Suker, Davor, 134
Sulemana, Kamaldeen, 119
Sullivan, Cavan, 143
Sundhage, Pia, 160, 187
Swanson, Mallory, 80, 126, 180, 187

Sweden, 13, 14, 22, 23, 24, 36, 37, 79, 92, 116, 139, 157, 169, 182, 184, 187, 188
Swiss cheese, 87
Switzerland, 12, 13, 27, 29, 36, 72, 103, **111**, **117**, 131, 184
Sydney, Australia, 76, 184, 188
Syria, 139

T

Tanikawa, Momoko, 160
Tanzania, 158
Tarciane, 160
technical staff, 49
Tel, Mathys, 143
televised matches, 5, 24, 45, 80, 90, 164
Telstar ball, 45, 75
Thompson, Alyssa, 126, 160, 174, 175
Thompson, Gisele, 160, 175
Tianhe Stadium, 24
ticker-tape parades, 29, 85
ticket sales, 9, 12, 16, 20, 21, 85, 98, 162
tifos, 84
tiki-taka style of play, 149
time wasting, 60, 87
tips and tricks from soccer pros, 196–199
toe poke, 55
Tokyo, Japan, 156, 184, 188
Toronto, Ontario, Canada, 98, 168, 171
totaalvoetbal ("total football"), 133
Tottenham Hotspur, 59, 135
traffic light, 50
training, 15, 35, 72, 79, 118–120, 196
Trinidad and Tobago, 140
Triple-Edged Sword, 24
Triple Espresso, 187
triumphant pose celebration, 69
truncated icosahedron, 45
Tshabalala, Siphiwe, 66
T-shirts, 38, 85, 90, 93, 97
Tunisia, **111**
tug of war, 182

turf, 3, 79
turf burn, 79
Turkey, 141, 143
Turner, Matt, 127
Twellman, Taylor, 78

U

UEFA (Union of European Football Associations), 103, 104, 106–111, 112–117, 141, 143, 179
umbrellas, 98
Umbro, 25
United Kingdom, 108, 113
United Nations, 13, 86
United States, **111**, **117**
unsporting behavior, 49
Uruguay, 4, 14, 15, 16, 17, 18, 26, 36, 54, 73, 99, 108, 109, **111**, 132, 184, 190
U.S. Soccer Federation
    legendary men's players, 128–131
    legendary women's players, 144–147
    players to watch, 122–127
    rules about heading for youth, 78

V

van Basten, Marco, 34, 80
Vancouver, British Columbia, Canada, 38, 98, 168
van Dijk, Virgil, 141, 198, 199
vanishing foam, 86
van Veenendaal, Sari, 152
VAR (Video Assistant Referee) review, 49, 62
Vatican City, 13
Vavá, 134
Vermeeren, Arthur, 143
video match officials, 62, 63
Vietnam, **117**, 126
Vinícius Júnior, 34, 142, 178
volley kick, 55
vuvuzelas, 83

W

Wales, 108, **111**, 182
Walsh, Keira, 180
Wambach, Abby, 39, 42, 71, 81, 147, 176, 189
warmups, 118, 196,
Weah, George, 34, 127
Weah, Tim, 127
wearing jewelry, 47, 62
Wembley Stadium, 21, 27, 185
Wen, Sun, 23, 25, 71, 148, 150
West Germany, 36, 67, 75, 90, 105, 133, 138, 184
whistle, 62
Whitham, McKenna "Mak," 161, 175
Widdowson, Sam Weller, 46, 47
Wiegmann, Bettina, 71
Wilkinson, Rhian, 187
Williams, Nico, 119, 185
Wilson, Sophia (formerly Smith), 97, 127, 152, 161, 173, 174, 176, 187
winning a house, 18
Wirtz, Florian, 143
Women's Professional Soccer (WPS), 121, 172, 176
Women's Super League (WSL), 180
Women's United Soccer Association (WUSA), 172, 176
Wondolowski, Chris, 170
World Cup attendance, 24, 38, 98–99
World Cup hosting, 2, 4, 28, 98, 162
World Cup revenue, 162–164
World Cup viewership (TV and streaming), 5, 164
World Cup Willie, 90, 98
World War I, 183
World War II, 4, 13, 26, 137, 183, 186
Wynalda, Eric, 131

Y

Yamal, Lamine, 97, 143, 185
Yashin, Lev, 136, **137**
Yedlin, DeAndre, 131
yellow cards, 50–52, 62, 191, 192
Yildiz, Kenan, 143
"yoga man," 119
Yohannes, Lily, 161
younger soccer talents
    men, 139–143
    women, 155–161

YouTube, 196
yo-yo tests, 62
Yugoslavia, 15, 16, 134, 138, 184

Z

Zaccardo, Cristian, 73
Zambia, 101, 102, **117**
Zanotti, Gabi, 103
Zidane, Zinedine, 34, 52, **53**, 132
Zidane pirouette, 53
Zmuda, Wladyslaw, 138

ABOUT THE AUTHOR

Emily J. Dolbear is the author of dozens of kids' books and the editor of many more. Reviewers have called her voice "cheeky and humorous," with content "painstakingly researched." Searching for answers to life's questions, big or small, drives her writing—just look at *The World Almanac Book of Why: Explanations for Absolutely Everything*. She might never have discovered all these incredible facts about the world's most popular sport were it not for two supporters of the game—her sons. When World Cup soccer rolls around, Emily and her family gather on a couch to watch the U.S. men's and women's teams, cheering as though they can change the outcome. She lives in Brookline, Massachusetts.